To Jim Bagla
with best
wishes!
[signature]
1984

Books by Ray Miller

Ray Miller's Galveston
Ray Miller's Houston
Eyes of Texas Travel Guide: Panhandle/Plains Edition
Eyes of Texas Travel Guide: Fort Worth/Brazos Valley Edition
Eyes of Texas Travel Guide: Hill Country/Permian Basin Edition
Eyes of Texas Travel Guide: San Antonio/Border Edition
Eyes of Texas Travel Guide: Dallas/East Texas Edition
Eyes of Texas Travel Guide: Houston/Gulf Coast Edition

RAY MILLER'S TEXAS PARKS

A History and Guide

RAY MILLER'S
TEXAS PARKS
A History and Guide

Copyright© 1984 by Ray Miller

All rights reserved under International and Pan-American Copyright Conventions. Published in the United States by Cordovan Press, A Division of Cordovan Corporation. First printing, October 1984

Library of Congress Catalog Card Number 84-72567
ISBN: 0-89123-046-7

Design: John Hillenbrand

Set in Century Book II by Diana Rankin and Pattie Churchfield. Printed in the United States of America by Capital Printing, Austin.

Many of the Texas state
parks are on lands donated to
the state. This book is dedicated
to the donors.

CONTENTS

Foreword XI

Introduction XIII

The Genesis 1

Reservations Policies and General Rules 7

Texas Parks, Color Photographs 11

Region I — Parks in West Texas and the Panhandle 29

Region II — Parks in North Central Texas 61

Region III — Parks in Northeast Texas 89

Region IV — Parks in Southeast Texas 125

Region V — Parks in San Antonio and the Hill Country 155

Region VI — Parks in South Texas 199

Index 230

Acknowledgments 231

Photo Credits 232

FOREWORD

Whether you're a visitor, newcomer or native Texan, this book will help you discover the magnificent diversity and beauty of our great state. Here you will find the keys to hundreds of exciting places to visit. From historic sites to campsites, Ray Miller has explored the superb system of parks and recreational facilities throughout Texas. He invites you to view parts of our history preserved in parks such as the San Jacinto Battleground, restored military forts and eighteenth-century Spanish missions. Or if your interest is in viewing the dramatic and varied landscapes of our state, you will find this a handy guide in searching out the physical splendor and natural phenomena found in places like the vast dunes of Monahans Sandhills State Park or the rugged country of Palo Duro Canyon.

Through the years, my family and I have enjoyed visiting many of the wonderful parks and recreational areas found in this book, from the lofty mountain peaks of far West Texas to the hundreds of miles of sun-drenched seashore on the Gulf Coast. I hope that readers will enjoy as much as we have the opportunity to travel our state, taking in the impressive views, wonderful lakes and forests, rolling prairies and desert flats as well as learning about the culture and heritage that are all a part of Texas.

I want to thank Ray Miller for unveiling this state to readers everywhere, with an expert eye, true devotion and understanding. Through his fascinating and insightful travel guides, he shares the excitement of Texas and has helped preserve its history and beauty. With this book on Texas parks, he has done it again.

Mark White
Governor of Texas
July 1984

INTRODUCTION

This is a history and guide to the parks in the Texas Parks and Wildlife Department system. Texas also has hundreds of county and municipal parks. A few of them are mentioned in this guide. The parks maintained in Texas by the National Park Service are mentioned in the comments concerning state parks in the same areas. But this is not a book about all the parks in Texas.

The number and quality of parks in the state system have increased so much in the past twenty years that many Texans may not be fully aware of what we have. I am convinced our state parks system is the equal of any system anywhere. I have written this book to convince you that you should go and see for yourself.

Ray Miller
Houston
July 1984

THE GENESIS

The state park system in Texas did not grow out of any master plan. There were parks before there were plans. The legislature ordered the purchase of the Alamo and the cemetery at the San Jacinto Battleground in 1883. Legislation in 1913 authorized the governor to accept donations of land at the Fannin Battleground Site in Goliad County. The acquisition of these historic sites was the actual beginning of the park system.

Isabella Neff gave the state six acres of land on the Leon River in Coryell County in 1913. This is often referred to as the original state park because it apparently inspired Gov. Pat Neff to ask the legislature in 1923 to establish a State Parks Board. The governor was Isabella Neff's son. He donated additional land for the Mother Neff State Park. The State Parks Board was authorized to solicit donations of land for parks. Fifty sites had been donated by 1926. The Parks Board did not have the money to develop them. Some never were developed. Thirty-one were developed during the 1930s in collaboration with the National Park Service, the Civilian Conservation Corps (CCC), Works Progress Administration (WPA) and National Youth Administration.

Federal programs for developing parks were part of the Franklin Roosevelt administration's New Deal. Most of the work was done by the CCC. The CCC was conceived as much to make work for young men as to conserve natural resources. It was one of the most successful New Deal agencies and one of President Roosevelt's personal favorites. Two and a half million young men spent some time in the CCC between 1933 and 1942. They lived in camps supervised by Army officers. They earned $30 a month and worked on many different projects all over the United States. Some of them built parks. The parks they built in Texas are some of the best parks we have. Most of the improvements the men of the CCC built are still in use. The CCC really put Texas in the parks business. The legislature expanded the authority of the Parks Board during the CCC years. The board was authorized to buy parks. No money was provided, but the board did contract to buy Longhorn Caverns and the Palo Duro Canyon Park site and pay for them out of anticipated park revenues.

The legislature created Goose Island State Park and Texas Canyons State

Park by appropriating state lands. The name of Texas Canyons Park was changed to Big Bend State Park in 1933. The state gave this park to the federal government in 1939 and it became the first national park in Texas. These were the exceptions. Most of the parks the state acquired between 1923 and 1960 were donated or leased.

The legislature was never generous with appropriations. Park managers were expected to get most of their income from park concessions. State parks were generally run down when the Parks Board, Texas Research League and Texas Tech started developing a long-range park program in 1960.

The State Parks Board and the older Game and Fish Commission were consolidated in 1963 into the present Parks and Wildlife Department. The department qualified for federal matching grants under the Land and Water Conservation program in 1965. The legislature and the voters approved a constitutional amendment in 1967 authorizing the department to issue revenue bonds to raise money for new parks. The department started charging entrance fees at most parks to pay off the bonds.

The legislature made more money available for parks in 1971 and 1978 by earmarking part of the cigarette tax for the Texas Park Fund and the Texas

Local Park, Recreation and Open Space Fund. New parks have been added to the system during the past few years at a faster rate than any time since the 1920s. There are now 121 parks in the system, with 24 more projected to be added by 1990. The parks were all referred to as state parks earlier. The department changed some of the designations in 1975. There are now 35 state parks, 40 state recreation areas, 3 state natural areas, 17 state historical parks, 19 state historic sites, 4 state historic structures and 3 state fishing piers in the system.

The Parks and Wildlife Department headquarters building is at 4200 Smith School Road in south Austin. The staff includes specialists trained in park planning, research, conservation, wildlife management, security, archaeology, architectural restoration and interior design. The Parks and Wildlife Department has 2,033 employees. Of these, 163 men and women work in the wildlife division at 22 wildlife management areas, 11 fish hatcheries and other fisheries divisions. Four hundred and fifty are game wardens. All the game wardens are peace officers with jurisdiction anywhere there is hunting or fishing. They also enforce the water safety laws. Some park personnel are peace officers and some are not.

Youth groups and families with young children still are partial to the shaded camp grounds of Mother Neff State Park, where Texans have been camping since the 1920s.

REGION I
PARKS IN WEST TEXAS AND THE PANHANDLE

1. Magoffin Home State Historic Site
2. Franklin Mountains State Park
3. Hueco Tanks State Historical Park
4. Fort Leaton State Historic Site
5. Davis Mountains State Park
6. Balmorhea State Recreation Area
7. Monahans Sandhills State Park
8. Fort Lancaster State Historic Site
9. Seminole Canyon State Historical Park
10. Fort McKavett State Historic Site
11. Lake Colorado City State Recreation Area
12. Big Spring State Recreation Area
13. Mackenzie State Recreation Area
14. Palo Duro Canyon State Park
15. Caprock Canyons State Park

REGION II
PARKS IN NORTH CENTRAL TEXAS

1. Acton State Historic Site
2. Dinosaur Valley State Park
3. Cleburne State Recreation Area
4. Jeff Davis State Recreation Area
5. Lake Whitney State Recreation Area
6. Meridian State Recreation Area
7. Mother Neff State Park
8. Lake Brownwood State Recreation Area
9. Abilene State Recreation Area
10. Fort Griffin State Historical Park
11. Copper Breaks State Park
12. Lake Arrowhead State Recreation Area
13. Fort Richardson State Historical Park
14. Possum Kingdom State Recreation Area
15. Lake Mineral Wells State Park

REGION III
PARKS IN NORTHEAST TEXAS

1. Eisenhower State Recreation Area
2. Eisenhower Birthplace State Historic Site
3. Bonham State Recreation Area
4. Sam Bell Maxey House State Historic Structure
5. Governor Hogg Shrine State Historical Park
6. Daingerfield State Park
7. Atlanta State Recreation Area
8. Caddo Lake State Park
9. Martin Creek Lake State Recreation Area
10. Tyler State Park
11. Jim Hogg State Historical Park
12. Rusk-Palestine State Park and Texas State Railroad Historical Park
13. Caddoan Mounds State Historic Site
14. Mission Tejas State Historical Park
15. Fairfield Lake State Recreation Area
16. Fort Parker State Recreation Area
17. Old Fort Parker State Historic Site
18. Confederate Reunion Grounds State Historical Park

REGION IV
PARKS IN SOUTHEAST TEXAS

1. San Jacinto Battleground Historical Park
2. Battleship Texas Historic Site
3. Galveston Island State Park
4. Bryan Beach State Recreation Area
5. Varner-Hogg Historical Park
6. Brazos Bend State Park
7. Stephen F. Austin Historical Park
8. Washington-on-the-Brazos Historical Park
9. Lake Somerville State Recreation Area
10. Huntsville State Park
11. Lake Livingston State Recreation Area
12. Cassells Boykin State Recreation Area
13. Martin Dies Jr. State Park
14. Sabine Pass Battleground Historical Park
15. Sea Rim State Park

REGION V
PARKS IN SAN ANTONIO AND THE HILL COUNTRY

1. San Jose Mission State Historic Site
2. Jose Antonio Navarro State Historic Site
3. Guadalupe River State Park
4. Palmetto State Park
5. Monument Hill-Kreische Brewery State Historic Site
6. Buescher State Park
7. Bastrop State Park
8. Lockhart State Recreation Area
9. McKinney Falls State Park
10. Longhorn Cavern State Park
11. Inks Lake State Park
12. Pedernales Falls State Park
13. Blanco State Recreation Area
14. Lyndon B. Johnson State Historical Park
15. Admiral Nimitz State Historical Park
16. Enchanted Rock State Natural Area
17. Kerrville State Recreation Area
18. Hill Country State Natural Area
19. Lost Maples State Natural Area
20. Garner State Park
21. Landmark Inn State Historic Site

REGION VI
PARKS IN SOUTH TEXAS

1. Lake Corpus Christi State Recreation Area
2. Lipantilan State Historic Site
3. Tips State Recreation Area
4. Goliad State Historical Park
5. Fannin Battleground State Historic Site
6. Lake Texana State Recreation Area
7. Port Lavaca State Fishing Pier
8. Matagorda Island State Park and Wildlife Management Area
9. Copano Bay State Fishing Pier
10. Fulton Mansion State Historic Structure
11. Goose Island State Recreation Area
12. Mustang Island State Park
13. Port Isabel Lighthouse Historic Structure
14. Queen Isabella State Fishing Pier
15. Brazos Island State Recreation Area
16. Bentsen-Rio Grande Valley State Park
17. Falcon State Recreation Area

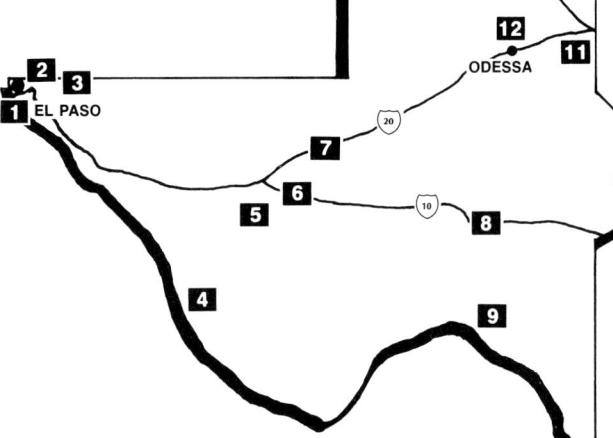

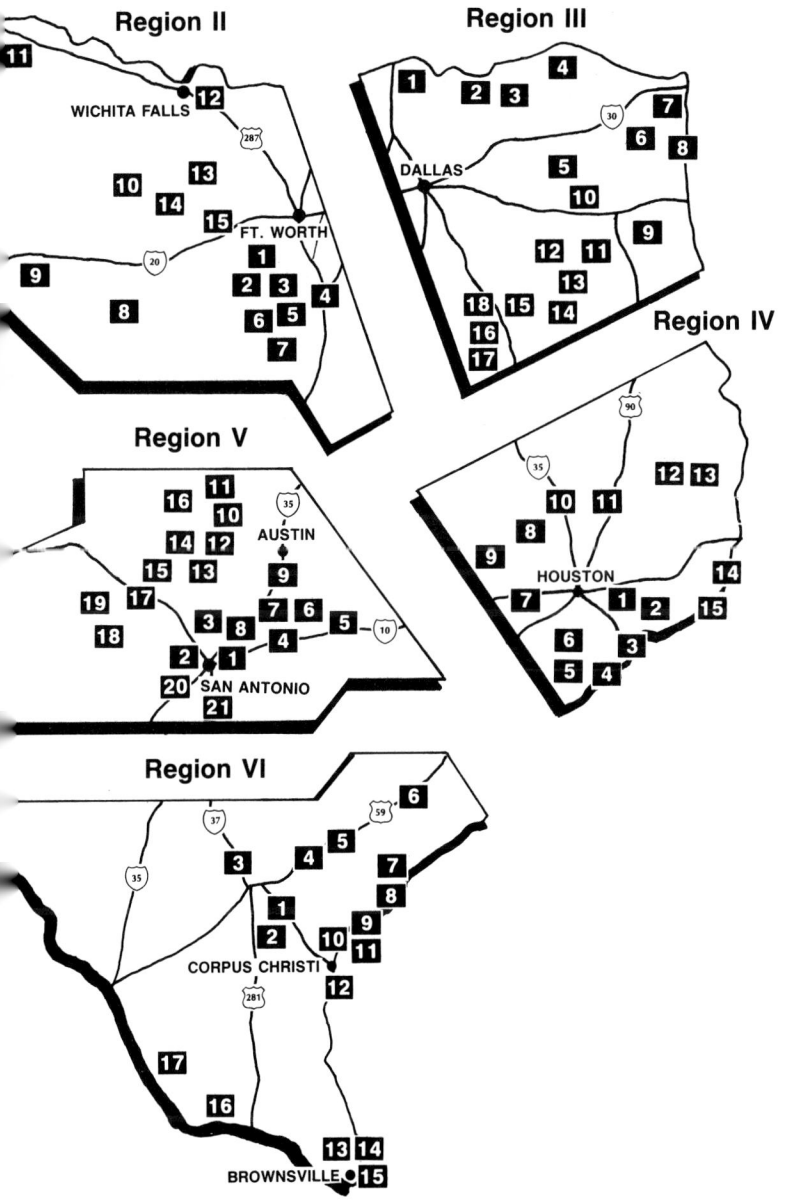

Texas Parks and Wildlife headquarters building at 4200 Smith School Road in Austin.

RESERVATIONS POLICIES AND GENERAL RULES

Many of the state parks with camping areas have group camps, group shelters or dining halls. These are in some demand for meetings and family reunions. The parks hold drawings every January 11 for the right to rent these premises on specific dates. Forms are available from the parks. Applicants list their first, second, third and fourth date choices. The forms must be filed between December 1 and January 10. The drawings on January 11 determine which groups get what dates during the year beginning February 1. A reservation fee in the amount of one day's fee is required when the results are announced.

Group camps and shelters can be reserved by phone or letter on any dates not claimed through the drawing. The rule on reservations not covered by the drawing is that they cannot be made more than 90 days ahead of the actual use date. This rule applies to all campsites, screened shelters and cabins. The Parks and Wildlife Department hopes eventually to have a central reservations system. Reservations must be made with the individual parks in the meantime. Their addresses and phone numbers are listed with the descriptions of the parks in this book. Reservation fees are required in certain situations.

Campers should pay their fees and pick up their permits at the park headquarters before they occupy a campsite. But they can occupy the site they have been assigned and check in with the office the next morning if they arrive after the park office has closed. Campers without reservations can claim vacant campsites and take care of the formalities the next morning if they arrive after the office has closed.

Checkout time for dining halls and group shelters rented for the day is 10 p.m. Checkout time for overnight campers is 2 p.m. Campers are limited to 14 consecutive days per visit. There are limits on the number of people permitted to occupy the dining halls, shelters, cabins and campsites. The limit for screened shelters and campsites usually is eight. The other limits vary.

Entrance fees are usually $2 per car. You can buy a restricted permit allowing you to use any one park as often as you like for a year for $8. You can buy an annual permit allowing you to use all the state parks for $15 a year. Senior citizens can get a Parklands Passport for no charge. It is good for the entrance fee at any park and also good for tour charges at most parks. Holders of the annual permits and the Parklands Passports pay the regular fees for camping, swimming and golfing. Permits and passports can be obtained at 4200 Smith School Road in Austin or at any park.

Cabins, shelters and campsites usually have parking space for two vehicles or one vehicle and one trailer. Extra vehicles have to be parked somewhere else. Some parks have designated areas where excess vehicles can be parked for a fee.

Some of the parks have trails that cannot be negotiated and attractions that cannot be reached by handicapped people. The buildings, restrooms and showers are equipped to accommodate the handicapped. Seeing-eye dogs are welcomed, but no pets are allowed in any park buildings and they are not allowed on park grounds unless they are leashed.

No alcoholic beverages are permitted to be sold in the state parks. All the parks have conspicuous signs prohibiting the public consumption of alcohol. "Public" is the operative word. They don't search your cooler.

Gathering firewood is prohibited in most parks most of the time. It is allowed if some trees have been cut or blown down, for instance. Bundles of firewood are sold in camp stores in a few parks. You should take your own wood if you are counting on a wood fire, unless you are sure the park you are headed for has wood available. Wood fires are prohibited in the primitive camping areas in most parks.

Rules against littering and loud music are included in the regulations posted in every park.

Motorcycles that are legal on the street are legal in the parks, but only on the roads. A few parks have areas set aside for mini-bikes. Street-legal and off-road motorcycles are not allowed on any biking or nature trail in any park.

Don't take your metal detector with you. You cannot use it in any state park. It is illegal to do any digging or pick up any artifacts or souvenirs such as rocks, petrified wood, plants, etc. in a state park.

Hunting is prohibited in most state parks. Fishing is under the same regulations as fishing anywhere else in Texas. You need a license unless you are under 17 or over 65. You can get licenses at most tackle shops. You can find out anything else you need to know about fishing regulations free by calling (800) 792-1112.

Identification of color photographs on the preceding pages.

P 11	Galveston Island State Park
P 12	*Above:* Copano Bay State Fishing Pier
	Below: Landmark Inn State Historic Site
P 13	Fort Lancaster State Historic Site
P 14	Texas State Railroad Historical Park
P 15	*Above:* Palmetto State Park
	Below: Lake Whitney State Recreation Area
P 16	Monahans Sandhills State Park
P 17	*Above:* Palo Duro Canyon State Park
	Below: Longhorn Cavern State Park
P 18	Seminole Canyon State Historical Park
P 19	*Above:* Mother Neff State Park
	Below: Goliad State Historical Park
P 20	Inks Lake State Park
P 21	*Above:* Fort Griffin State Historical Park
	Below: Pedernales Falls State Park
P 22	Caprock Canyons State Park
P 23	*Above:* Lost Maples State Natural Area
	Below: Jim Hogg State Historical Park
P 24	Davis Mountains State Park
P 25	Old Fort Parker State Historic Site
P 26	Caddo Lake State Park

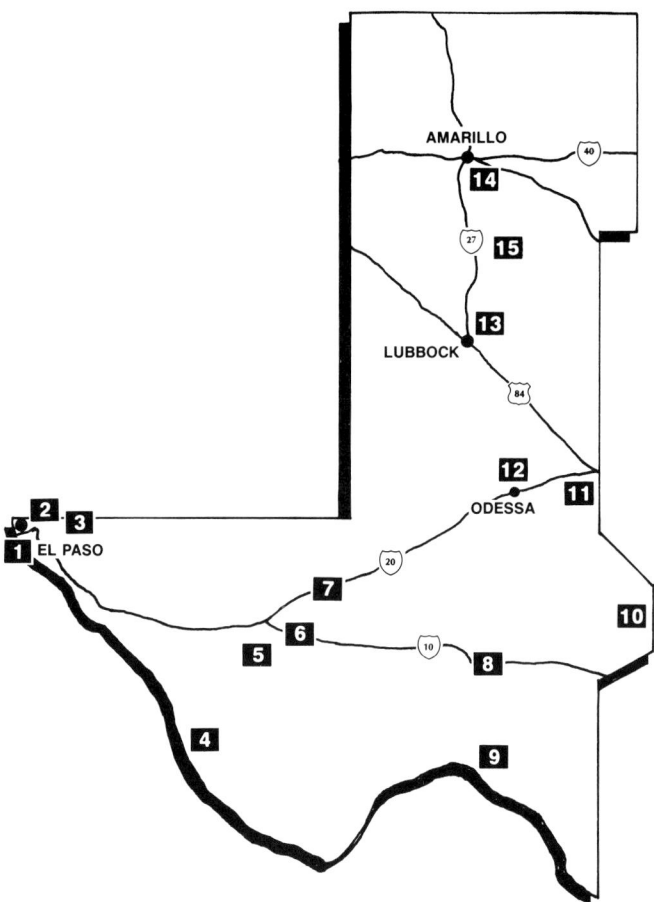

1. Magoffin Home State Historic Site
2. Franklin Mountains State Park
3. Hueco Tanks State Historical Park
4. Fort Leaton State Historic Site
5. Davis Mountains State Park
6. Balmorhea State Recreation Area
7. Monahans Sandhills State Park
8. Fort Lancaster State Historic Site
9. Seminole Canyon State Historical Park
10. Fort McKavett State Historic Site
11. Lake Colorado City State Recreation Area
12. Big Spring State Recreation Area
13. Mackenzie State Recreation Area
14. Palo Duro Canyon State Park
15. Caprock Canyons State Park

REGION I
PARKS IN WEST TEXAS AND THE PANHANDLE

This area is about one-third of the state, but it has fewer than one-fifth of the state parks. The state parks are really spaced out, but there are three major national parks in this area.

El Paso is the biggest city in West Texas and the fourth biggest city in Texas. The list of parks in this region begins with El Paso. The numbers are just for convenience and reference purposes. I have not attempted to rank the parks. But my own favorite in this section is Davis Mountains State Park because of the accommodations and the climate.

Parks Under Development

There is just one park under development in this region. The tentative name is South Llano River Park. It is the former Warner Buck Ranch, south of Junction in Kimble County. It is approximately 2,600 acres. Buck donated it in 1977.

MAGOFFIN HOME STATE HISTORIC SITE

Magoffin Street between Octavia and Noble, 7 blocks east of the Federal Courthouse in downtown El Paso.
Fees: adults $1, children 25¢

El Paso is not an ancient city. The town on the other side of the Rio Grande is older. It is called Juarez now. It was originally called Paso del Norte. The present city of El Paso grew out of several small settlements. The growth really began after the California gold rush started in 1849. The town was called Franklin from 1852 until 1859. It has been called El Paso since then. El Paso was incorporated in 1873. One of the incorporators built this house in 1875. He was Joseph Magoffin.

The Magoffins were here a long time before 1875. James and Maria Magoffin settled near here in 1849. James was a merchant. A little settlement grew up around his home and store and warehouse. The settlement was called Magoffinsville. The original Fort Bliss was at Magoffinsville. The settlement and most of the fort were destroyed when the Rio Grande flooded in 1868. James Magoffin died a short time later. His son Joseph carried on the family business and branched out into banking and politics. Joseph Magoffin served four terms as mayor of El Paso and held several other local offices.

The house Joseph built is now on the edge of the business district. It was on the outskirts of town when he built it and it was surrounded then by acres of gardens and orchards.

The Magoffin house was a major social center in El Paso in the late 1800s. The original building had six rooms. The house was expanded twice between 1875 and 1887. It now has 20 rooms. The style is called Territorial. It is a Spanish colonial adobe with some details borrowed from the Greek Revival style. The house has been occupied by Magoffins since it was built. Joseph's daughter inherited the house. Her daughter, Octavia Magoffin Glasgow, still lives in one wing.

The remainder of the Magoffin house is open for tours Wednesdays through Sundays from 9 a.m. till 4 p.m. The guided tours take about an hour. Many of the Magoffin family's furnishings are still in the house. The house and furnishings were bought by the city of El Paso and the Parks and Wildlife Department in 1976.

The fees for the guided tours are $1 for adults and 25 cents for children, 6 to 12. You should make arrangements in advance for group tours.

For more information

You can arrange tours or get more information about this house by writing to the Superintendent, Magoffin Home State Historic Site, 1120 Magoffin Avenue, El Paso, TX 79901 or by calling (915) 533-5147.

Other places to see

Other places you may want to see in this area are the city of Juarez, biggest of the Mexican border towns; the Fort Bliss Museum off U.S. 54 in northeast El Paso; the Cavalry Museum, I-10 at Loop 375; Hueco Tanks State Historical Park, 32 miles east on Ranch Road 2775 north of U.S. 180; the old church and the Tigua Indian Reservation at Ysleta, State Highway 20 in southeast El Paso; the mission at Socorro on F.M. 258 just south of the city; and the Viceroy's Palace at San Elizario, just down the river from Socorro.

The Magoffin home was built in 1875 in what is now downtown El Paso for one of the area's pioneer families. It is an unusual combination of Spanish colonial and Greek Revival architectural features.

FRANKLIN MOUNTAINS STATE PARK

Between north El Paso city limits and New Mexico border, north and south of State Highway Loop 275. No fees

This park covers 24,000 acres, and more acreage may be added. The Parks and Wildlife Department acquired the land from the city and county of El Paso and from several individuals. No improvements have been made. The roads on the property are not considered safe; so no vehicles are allowed in the park.

The park is open for hiking and picnicking. Visitors can enter from Loop 275. They do not have to bother with formalities. There is no entrance, no headquarters, no staff and no entrance fee.

Visitors can picnic where they please, but they will find no tables. There are no provisions for camping, but there is no prohibition against it either.

The park offers plenty of wide open space and nothing else. Visitors planning to stay more than a couple of hours should bring with them everything they expect to need. Reservations are not necessary.

For more information

More information can be obtained from the Superintendent, Hueco Tanks State Historical Park, Rt. 3, Box 1, Hueco Tanks Road, El Paso, TX 79935. The phone number is (915) 859-4100.

Other places to see

Other places of interest nearby are the Cavalry Museum, I-10 at Loop 375; Fort Bliss Museum off U.S. 54 in northeast El Paso; aerial tramway, Ranger Peak, McKinley and Piedras, in northwest El Paso; Magoffin Home State Historic Site, 1120 Magoffin Avenue; and Tigua Indian Reservation, State Highway 20 in southeast El Paso.

Left: The Franklin Mountains State Park is a vast wilderness just north of the El Paso city limits. No vehicles are allowed.

Opposite: This is one of the places the Indians and early travelers stopped for water. The water at most of the water stops in the West came from springs. The water here is rainwater, captured in natural rock basins.

HUECO TANKS STATE HISTORICAL PARK

32 miles east of El Paso on Ranch Road 2775 north of U.S. 180 in El Paso County. Entrance fee: $2 per car

A mass of molten rock pushed up into the earth's crust here 34 million years ago. It cooled and hardened. The softer rock around it weathered away and three islands of hard rock the geologists call syenite porphyry were left exposed. There were forests here thousands of years ago, but the area is desert now. The rock mountains have a number of depressions in their surfaces. These hollows catch and hold water during the occasional rains. So this was a very important place before windmills.

There is evidence that Indians visited here 10,000 years ago. Some Pueblo people apparently lived here around 1,000 A.D. They left some pictographs on the rocks. The Mescalero Apaches camped here in the 1700s and they left some art behind, too.

The early Spanish explorers did not come this way. The Spanish probably did not hear about the tanks until the late 1600s when they were starting their set-

tlements on the Rio Grande. The Spanish provided the name. *Hueco* is their word for hollow. The area around Hueco Tanks was originally granted to the Tigua Indians.

The Butterfield-Overland Mail line had a way station here in the 1850s. The ruins of the building are still here. The tanks were part of the Silverio Escontrias ranch from 1898 until 1956. El Paso County bought the land in 1965 and gave it to the state in 1969. The park opened in 1970.

Water was the main attraction for the Indians here. The paintings the Indians left behind are the main attraction for modern visitors. There are paintings on all three of the stone mountains. An interpretative trail leads to some of the paintings; a hiking trail goes to some of the others. One hundred and fifty species of birds have been sighted here, including golden eagles and prairie falcons. Grey foxes, bobcats and mountain lions visit occasionally.

The park has 43 individual picnic sites with shade shelters and 14 without shelters. There are 20 campsites with water, electricity, table and grill at $6 a night. Twelve of the campsites have shade shelters. The restrooms have showers. There is a playground and a sanitary dump — many more comforts than the passengers on the Butterfield stage found here.

For more information

You can reserve campsites or get more information by writing the Superintendent, Hueco Tanks State Historical Park, Rt. 3, Box 1, Hueco Tanks Road, El Paso, TX 79935. The phone number is (915) 859-4100.

Other places to see

This is the state campground closest to the Guadalupe Mountains National Park, which is 90 miles east on U.S. 180. People from somewhere else may not think a place 90 miles away is close. West Texans think nothing of a 90-mile drive.

Other places to visit in this area are the city of Juarez across the river from El Paso; Magoffin Home State Historic Site, 1120 Magoffin Street in El Paso; Fort Bliss Museum off U.S. 54 in northeast El Paso; and the Tigua Indian Reservation off State Highway 20 in southeast El Paso.

Left: There are some old Indian pictographs at Hueco Tanks and some early American graffiti, too. Travelers in pioneer days scratched their names and occasional messages here on what is known as Newspaper Rock.

Opposite: The staff at Fort Leaton State Historic Site can handle tour groups of up to 40 people. Advance reservations are not required but they are advised for large groups.

FORT LEATON STATE HISTORIC SITE

4 miles southeast of Presidio in Presidio County.
Fees: adults $1, children 25¢

This was still Indian country after the war between the United States and Mexico ended in 1848. The United States got all the territory between here and the Pacific under the terms of the treaty and the United States agreed to try to keep the Comanches from raiding across the Rio Grande. The U.S. Army built several forts along the border to try to discourage Indian raids into Mexico. A private citizen built this fort. Some said his purpose was to encourage Indian raids into Mexico.

Ben Leaton had been a bounty hunter in Mexico before he settled here in 1848. He collected Indian scalps and sold them to the Mexican government. Leaton gave up bounty hunting and started trading with the Indians when he came here. He furnished them guns and ammunition and anything else they needed in exchange for cattle he presumably knew the Indians had stolen in Mexico. There were serious risks involved in this line of work and nobody knew this better than Ben Leaton.

He built a strong adobe wall around his headquarters and it has been called Fort Leaton ever since. The compound included a horse corral and 40 rooms. It was said to be the biggest adobe complex ever built in Texas. Leaton built it on a low bluff above the Rio Grande and it served its purpose. The unpopular proprietor

lived here safely for three years and died of natural causes in 1851.

Leaton's widow married customs agent Edward Hall. He mortgaged the fort to John Burgess. Hall could not pay off the mortgage. Burgess foreclosed. Hall refused to move out. He soon turned up dead. Burgess moved his family into the fort and carried on a freighting business between San Antonio and Chihuahua for 11 years until he was murdered.

The Burgess family continued to live here until 1926. The fort was abandoned then and it was falling down by the 1930s. Some local people raised money to repair it, but it was falling down again in 1968 when Frank Skidmore donated it to the state.

The Parks and Wildlife Department has rebuilt the old fort with adobe bricks handmade on the site. It's probably in better shape than it ever was when Ben Leaton was here. It is open to visitors every day. The fee for the guided tour is $1 for adults and 25 cents for children, 6 to 12.

There are three picnic shelters on the grounds. There is no campground.

For more information

You can get more information about the Fort Leaton State Historic Site from the Superintendent, P.O. Box 1220, Presidio, TX 79845. The phone number is (915) 229-3613.

Other places to see

The best thing about Fort Leaton is its location. State Highway 170 is one of the most scenic drives in Texas. It runs on down the border from here to Lajitas and the western entrance to Big Bend National Park. The Big Bend entrance is 64 miles from Fort Leaton. Big Bend is the oldest national park in Texas. The state legislature gave the National Park Service the first 250,000 acres of land in 1934 along with $1.5 million to pay for additional land. The park now covers 708,221 acres of mountains and desert. Raft trips on the Rio Grande can be arranged at Lajitas and Terlingua.

The Davis Mountains get a little more moisture than the rest of West Texas. The altitude is 5,000 feet; the climate is mild. The park has some spacious campgrounds, a lodge and 25 picnic sites for day visitors.

DAVIS MOUNTAINS STATE PARK

On State Highway 118, 4 miles northwest of Fort Davis in Jeff Davis County. Entrance fee: $2 per car

The U.S. Army started building military posts along the road to California after the gold strike in 1849. West Texas was still Indian country. Wagon trains and stage coaches needed protection. Six companies of the 8th Infantry under Lt. Col. Washington Seawell came here to Limpia Canyon in the fall of 1854 and established a base they named Fort Davis.

The base was named for Jefferson Davis because he was Secretary of War at the time. The troops patrolled the area and skirmished with the Comanches and Apaches and escorted travelers until Texas seceded from the Union in 1861. The Union troops withdrew then. A Confederate cavalry brigade was stationed here for a few months, but the fort was abandoned during most of the Civil War. The Indians destroyed most of the buildings.

Federal troops returned to Fort Davis in 1867. They rebuilt the post at the present site and the fort was manned continually until 1891. Quanah Parker's Comanches had been forced onto a reservation in Oklahoma and Geronimo's Apaches

had been defeated and captured by that time. There was no longer any need for the fort. The troops left. The government had never bought the land. It had been leased from John James; so it went back to the James estate. The stone and adobe buildings began to crumble. Prickly pears grew up around them. Fort Davis was the most picturesque ruined fort in North America in the 1950s. Congress declared it a National Historic Site in 1961 and appropriated the money to buy it and restore it.

Jefferson Davis was president of the Confederacy during the Civil War. He was jailed and charged with treason after Lee surrendered. He had just been released from jail on bond (President Andrew Johnson would later pardon him) when Union troops returned to the fort in Limpia Canyon. It would not have been surprising if the Army had changed the name of the fort under the circumstances, but Texans made sure the name of the leader of the lost cause would be remembered here, whatever the Army did about the name of the fort. The town outside the fort had been named Fort Davis and nothing was going to change that. The mountains were named for Davis. The county was named for him when it was separated from Presidio County in 1887. And this park was named for the mountains named for him. I don't think there is another county in the state where so many places have been named for the same man, but we had only one Confederacy and it had only one president.

One of several small courtyards in the Indian Lodge, designed to resemble a pueblo, and built by the CCC in the 1930s.

The Davis Mountains State Park is in a valley near the head of Limpia Canyon, right next to the Fort Davis National Historic Site. The park covers 1,869 acres. About 500 acres were donated by ranchers J.W. Espy, J.W. Merrill and R.K. Merrill in the 1930s. The state purchased 793 areas in 1983; the rest of the land is leased.

The CCC did its most inspired work here. The principal improvement was an adobe lodge built to resemble an Indian pueblo. The original building had 16 rooms complete with rustic furniture, also built by the men of the CCC. The lodge has been maintained and expanded. There are now 39 very comfortable rooms with incomparable views. There is a heated pool and a restaurant. The lodge is air conditioned, but this is not really necessary. The climate here is the best in Texas — mild in winter, cool in summer.

The room rates at Indian Lodge are $22 a night for a single, $25 for a double, $30 for a double with two double beds, and $32 for a suite with two double beds. There is an additional charge of $4 a night for each extra adult, $1 for each additional child, 6 to 12. Children under 6 are free.

The lodge is open the year around except for the two weeks following the second Monday in January. It is very popular and you need reservations. You can make them by writing the Indian Lodge Manager, Box 786, Fort Davis, TX 78734 or by calling (915) 426-3254. Get in the original section if you can, and bring money. They do not take credit cards.

Nature lovers will find plenty of outdoor accommodations. The park has 42 tent campsites at $4 a night; 19 campsites with water, electricity, table and grill for $6 a night; and 27 sites with water, electricity, sewer connections, table and grill at $7 a night.

An interpretive center offers a view of a wildlife watering station. There is an amphitheater where park rangers put on programs about Indian lore and the natural history of the area. There is a mountain hiking trail and a scenic drive to the top of a mountain overlooking the town and the old fort. Campers should come prepared for cool nights. They are apt to need blankets, summer and winter.

For more information

You can reserve campsites or get more information by calling (915) 426-3337 or by writing the Superintendent, Davis Mountains State Park, Box 786, Fort Davis, TX 79734.

Other places to see

You can take the hiking trail to the old fort or you can drive there. The entrance fee is $1 per car. You can visit the University of Texas McDonald Observatory, 13 miles west of the park on State Highway 118, but they are very particular about when you can take a look at the heavens. They allow outsiders to do that only on the last Wednesday night of each month and only if they have made arrangements in advance, in writing, with the Visitors' Center, McDonald Observatory, Box 1337, Fort Davis, TX 79734. The drive west on State Highway 118 to the junction with State Highway 166 and left on 166 back around to Fort Davis will give you a good look at the Davis Mountains. Highway 166 will take you past the historic Bloys Campground, where members of the old ranching families still hold religious camp meetings for one week every summer as they have since 1889.

You will pass a vineyard and a winery on 166, too. Some of the stores in Fort Davis sell the wines produced at the Glasscock Vineyards.

BALMORHEA STATE RECREATION AREA

On old U.S. 290, 6 miles south of I-10 in Reeves County, halfway between Fort Stockton and Van Horn.
Entrance fee: $2 per car

The centerpiece in this park is the biggest natural spring in Texas. The land is owned by the Balmorhea Livestock Company and the Reeves County Water Improvement District No. 1. The state leases the 48 acres immediately surrounding the spring. This arrangement goes back to 1933. The original improvements in the park were conceived by the National Park Service and built by the CCC. The spring was turned into a swimming pool. It is one of the biggest in the country. It covers one and three-quarter acres and it is 30 feet deep in some places. There are aquatic plants and fish in it. The temperature of the water stays around 76 degrees. There is a natural circulation system. The spring flows 22 to 26 million gallons of water a day. The water flows out of the pool into a canal and then it is used for irrigation.

Indians found this spring thousands of years ago. No one now knows what they called it. Anglos used to call it Mescalero Spring because the Mescalero Apaches were making regular stops here during the early stages of the struggle for the West. Mexican farmers were the first to use the waters for irrigation. They called the springs San Solomon. Local people often use the pool and the picnic grounds here. The campground and the courts are popular with travelers visiting Big Bend, Fort Davis and Carlsbad. Most of the interstate travelers on I-10 never dream there is such a place here.

The CCC built a motel in this park in 1940. It has been renovated and the 18 rooms are modern and comfortable. The architecture is Spanish. The atmosphere is tranquil and pleasant. The rooms all have heat, air conditioning and television. Some have kitchenettes. Linens are furnished. Kitchen utensils are not. The rates at San Solomon Springs Courts are $20 for the first adult plus $4 for each additional adult and $1 for each additional child. There is an extra charge for kitchenettes. You can't beat this deal.

Shaded picnic sites surround the swimming pool. There are six campsites with shade shelters, tables and grills at $4 a night and 28 campsites with shelters, tables, grills, water and electricity at $6 a night. The restrooms in the campground have showers. There is a sanitary dump station and a playground.

The swimming pool has a modern bathhouse and concession stand. The pool fees are $1 for adults and 50 cents for children. The pool is open only during the summer — from the fourth Friday in May through Labor Day. The park and San Solomon Springs Courts are open year-round.

For more information

You can make reservations or get more information by writing the Superintendent, Balmorhea State Recreation Area, Box 15, Toyavale, TX 79786 or by calling (915) 375-2370.

Other places to see

You may also want to see Fort Davis National Historic Site and Davis Mountains State Park, 32 miles south on State Highway 17, and McDonald Observatory on Mount Locke, 46 miles southwest on State Highway 118.

Opposite Left: The campground in Balmorhea State Recreation Area has a view of the Davis Mountains. There is little natural shade here but there are plenty of shaded picnic shelters.

Left: Divers as well as swimmers enjoy the big pool at Balmorhea State Recreation Area. There are aquatic plants and fish in the deep areas of the pool. Balmorhea has a nice Spanish sound but it doesn't mean anything. Three early real estate promoters named Balcom, Morrow and Rhea created the word by combining their names.

MONAHANS SANDHILLS STATE PARK

Off I-20, 6 miles northeast of Monahans on the line between Ward and Winkler counties, 30 miles southwest of Odessa. Entrance fee: $2 per car

The contrast between this park and the one at Balmorhea will destroy any conception you may have had about West Texas being monotonous. The attraction at Balmorhea is the biggest spring in Texas. The attraction here is a sea of sand dunes like something out of a Foreign Legion movie. We have here nearly 4,000 acres of sand.

The people of Ward and Winkler counties promoted this park. They formed the Monahans Sandhills Park Association in the 1950s and started talking to the Sealy-Smith Foundation of Galveston. The foundation owned the land and still owns most of it. The Park Association obtained a deed to 320 acres and a long lease on another 3,520 acres. The association and Ward County leased the entire tract to the State Parks Board in 1956. The park opened in the fall of 1957. The local group raised the money to pay for the headquarters and visitor center. This building has windows looking out on an area where desert animals and birds come to feed and drink.

The Spanish discovered these dunes about 400 years ago, but did not take much interest in them. They probably didn't know and the first Anglos didn't know, either, that there is plenty of water here. The Indians discovered thousands of years ago that they could dig down a foot or two in the sand between the dunes and find fresh water. But there is not much you can do with fields of sand dunes, even with water. The area was of interest only to Indians until the first railroad came in the 1880s. The Permian Basin oil discoveries in the 1920s and 30s made every area out here interesting, but no way has been discovered yet to make sand dunes useful. They do make an unusual park.

Some of the dunes here are anchored by a tiny species of oak called Havard shinoak, but many of the dunes are shifting and moving with the wind and they look different every day. Most children enjoy the dunes. Adults may see all they

want to see in a few hours. There is a campground if you want to stay overnight. There are eight campsites with water, table and shelter at $4 a night and 20 sites with water, electricity, table and shelter at $6 a night. Some of the 28 picnic tables have shade shelters. Daytime temperatures get very warm here in the summer, but it is fairly comfortable in the shade. Nighttime temperatures are cool, even in July. Morning is the best time of day all over West Texas.

For more information

The address for reservations or more information is Superintendent, Monahans Sandhills State Park, Box 1738, Monahans, TX 79756. The phone number is (915) 943-2092.

Other places to see

Odessa is only half an hour away on I-20. Midland is about an hour away. These two cities have benefitted more than any others from the Permian Basin oil. They usually rank near the top among Texas cities in per capita income. Midland has four museums: the County Historical Museum in the county library building at 302 West Missouri; the Haley Library and History Center at 1805 West Indiana; the Museum of the Southwest at 1705 West Missouri; and the Permian Basin Petroleum Museum at 1500 I-20. Odessa has the Permian Basin branch of the University of Texas and Odessa College. Plays are presented at a replica of Shakespeare's Globe Theater at Odessa College.

Opposite Left: Most of the land in this park is leased from the Sealy-Smith Foundation of Galveston, established by the heirs of the late John Sealy to support John Sealy Hospital. Dunebuggies are no longer allowed here, but a concessionaire does rent sand surfboards.

Left: The endless sand vistas here are broken only by the occasional clumps of miniature oak trees. The dune field is much larger than the park. It extends beyond the New Mexico border.

FORT LANCASTER STATE HISTORIC SITE

On old U.S. 290, 5 miles southeast of Sheffield, 41 miles west of Ozona in Crockett County. No fee

The Apaches and the Comanches controlled West Texas when Americans started swarming across this state to get to California after the gold strike in 1849. One of the popular routes crossed the Pecos River near here; so this was a logical place for a fort when the U.S. Army started building a line of forts to protect the travelers.

Two companies of the 1st Infantry established the original camp here in August, 1855. The troops originally were quartered in shacks and temporary buildings. These were gradually replaced with stone buildings. Fort Lancaster had 25 permanent buildings by 1860. There was a stage station here and traffic moving through all the time. Troopers from Fort Lancaster rode with groups of travelers to Fort Stockton and then returned here. They did not chase Indians the way soldiers often do in the movies. They were not cavalrymen. They were infantrymen mounted on mules. They could not match the Indians in speed or horsemanship; so they relied on firepower, numbers and intimidation.

U.S. troops left the frontier forts when Texas seceeded from the Union in 1861. Some of the forts were reactivated after the war and some new forts were built as travelers shifted to other routes. There were a few troops at Fort Lancaster occasionally in the late 1860s, but the fort never was fully occupied again. The buildings have all fallen down. Only a few chimneys and fragments of walls still stand.

Crockett County gave the site to the Parks and Wildlife Department in 1968. The department has built nothing but a visitor center and a parking lot and does not plan any restoration. There is no fee here and there are no guides. There are two picnic tables with no shade. There are no campsites and there won't be any unless the department acquires more land. The park is just 82 acres.

The State Building Commission and Southern Methodist University did an archaeological survey here in 1966 and many of the artifacts uncovered are on display in the visitor center. There are coins, military insignia, buttons, silverware and bits of harness. The exhibits in the center also include photographs and a model

Fort Lancaster State Historic Site covers just under 83 acres. Amateur treasure-hunting is strictly forbidden.

of the fort the way it looked in its heyday. The ruins are all labelled and visitors are free to walk around the site and inspect what is left. Some people like restorations better. I like ruins. I hope this one is never restored.

For more information

There is not anything here to be reserved, but you can get more information about the Fort Lancaster State Historic Site by writing to the Superintendent at Box 306, Sheffield, TX 79781 or by calling (915) 836-4391.

Other places to see

Drive east on old 290 to the roadside park on top of the first mountain and look back towards the fort and beyond if you want to get some appreciation of the spirit and courage people had to have to venture out here in the 1850s.

There is not a state park campground within 100 miles of Fort Lancaster. There are commercial campgrounds at Fort Stockton and at the Caverns of Sonora, west of Sonora. The Circle Bar Truck Corral just east of Ozona has a motel that will improve your opinion of truck stops.

SEMINOLE CANYON STATE HISTORICAL PARK

On U.S. 90, 45 miles northwest of Del Rio in Val Verde County.
Entrance fee: $2 per car

The Seminoles contributed nothing to this place except the name. The canyon was probably named by the troops at Fort Clarke. They had some Seminole Indians working for them as scouts when they were trying to cope with the Comanches and Apaches here. The Seminoles had come to Texas from Florida and they never lived in canyons.

Seminole Canyon derives its fame from the efforts of a much earlier tribe. We do not know a lot about them, but they lived in the shallow limestone caves in these canyons along the Rio Grande 8,000 years ago. They did a little hunting, they ate roots and native plants, and they learned to make paint. That evidently was the thing they did best. Their paint has lasted a long time. Pictographs painted on the walls and ceilings of these rock shelters between 2,000 and 8,000 years ago are still here. They are the reason for this park.

The rock paintings in the canyons attracted occasional sightseers and vandals over the years. Many more visitors were attracted to the area after Amistad Lake was completed in 1968. The Parks and Wildlife Department bought 1,500 acres of land here in 1974 and another 700 acres in 1977 to create a park where the paintings can be enjoyed and still be protected. The park opened in 1980.

Visitors can go down into the canyon only with park rangers. They conduct tours twice a day, five days a week. The canyon is closed Mondays and Tuesdays. Tours are conducted at 10 a.m. and 3 p.m. Wednesdays through Sundays. They leave from the visitor center on the edge of the canyon. The visitor center has several handsome exhibits explaining the history of the canyon and what is known about the early inhabitants. The hike down into the canyon and back takes about an hour and a half. There is considerable climbing and people in poor physical condition should skip it. The park entrance fee covers the canyon tour.

A second hiking trail here leads to a cliff overlooking the Rio Grande. It is about 3.5 miles long and you guide yourself. The park has nine picnic sites with shade

Left: Seminole Canyon's best known pictograph is this red panther on the back wall of Panther Cave, but most visitors do not see it. Panther Cave is reachable now only by boat.

Opposite: Visitors are allowed in the rock shelters in Seminole Canyon only in the company of park rangers.

shelters near the visitor center. There are 31 camping sites with tables, shelters and water at $4 a night.

For more information

You can make reservations or get more information by calling (915) 292-4464 or by writing the Park Superintendent, Seminole Canyon State Historic Park, Box 806, Comstock, TX 78837. The phone number is (915) 292-4464.

Other places to see

The first southern transcontinental rail line was completed in 1883 when crews building the Southern Pacific tracks toward the east and crews building the Galveston, Harrisburg and San Antonio toward the west met near here. The railroad created the town of Langtry. A cantankerous justice of the peace named Roy Bean made Langtry famous. The highway department maintains a visitors center at the site where Judge Bean dispensed beer and whiskey and his brand of justice. It is about 25 miles northwest of here off U.S. 90. There is no state park at Amistad Lake, but the National Park Service maintains a number of recreation areas around the lake with free boat ramps, picnic areas and campsites. Accommodations of almost any kind are available in Del Rio. The lake is one of our finest. It has brought a lot of new people and new motels to this old border town.

FORT MCKAVETT STATE HISTORIC SITE

F.M. 1674 at F.M. 864, 40 miles northwest of Junction in Menard County. No fee

The U.S. Army established this fort on the Indian frontier in 1852 to protect settlers and travelers. It was named for Capt. Henry McKavett. He was one of the Americans killed in the Battle of Monterrey in 1846. The garrison here provided escorts for travelers until 1859. The frontier had moved farther west by that time and Fort McKavett was abandoned. The Indians pushed the frontier eastward during the Civil War. People did not feel safe here after the war; so the Army ordered troops back to Fort McKavett in 1867. They stayed until 1883. The famous Indian fighter, Ranald Mackenzie, was the commanding officer here once. Col. Abner Doubleday was in charge for a while, also.

Gen. William Sherman visited here during the 1871 frontier inspection tour that inspired him to declare war on the Comanches.

The Indians and the elements made a wreck of this fort after the Army left the first time in 1859. The buildings were all rebuilt after 1867. They were in good shape when the soldiers left for the last time in 1883. The government never had owned the land; so it went back to the owners. A small town developed. Some of the buildings were sold. Some were taken down or allowed to fall down. Some were occupied or used for storage right up until the Parks and Wildlife Department took over. Part of the land here was donated to the Parks and Wildlife Department in 1968 and the department has been buying up small parcels of land here ever since. Most of the fort site is included in the park now and the parks department has negotiated with the highway department to get the highway rerouted so it goes around the fort instead of through it.

Fourteen buildings are standing. Some others are being restored. Some of the ruined buildings will not be restored. The park is open while the development is going on. Some artifacts found on the grounds here are on exhibit in the small

The buildings of Fort McKavett were a welcome sight to travelers in the 1850s. The ruin in the foreground was once the commanding officer's residence.

museum in the restored hospital building. Visitors are free to walk around and look at the buildings and ruins. There is no guided tour, no campground, and no entrance fee. There are picnic tables on the grounds.

For more information

You can get more information from the Superintendent, Fort McKavett State Historic Site, Box 867, Fort McKavett, TX 76841. The phone number is (915) 396-2358.

Other places to see

Nearby are the Caverns of Sonora, 46 miles southwest off I-10 west of Sonora, and the ruins of the eighteenth-century San Saba Presidio in the county park at Menard, 23 miles northeast.

LAKE COLORADO CITY STATE RECREATION AREA

On F.M. 2836, south of I-20, 11 miles southwest of Colorado City in Mitchell County. Entrance fee: $2 per car

Texas Electric Service Company created this lake by damming Morgan Creek in 1949 to get cooling water for a power plant. The Morgan Creek generating plant is the biggest power plant in West Texas.

The power company gave Colorado City 500 acres of land on the lake. The city built a park and then gave it to the Parks and Wildlife Department in 1970. Fishing, swimming and skiing are the main attractions here. The park has more than five miles of lake frontage. There is a boat ramp, a swimming beach and two fishing piers. The warm water agrees with the native bass and catfish. The lake covers 1,618 acres.

The park has 53 campsites with water, table and grill at $4 a night; 20 sites with water, electricity, table and grill at $6 a night and 27 sites with full hookups at $7 a night. There is a prairie dog town and an area set aside for mini-bikes.

Birdwatchers can score here, especially in the winter when many migratory waterfowl visit the lake.

Colorado City was one of the first real boom towns in West Texas. The town was created by the Texas and Pacific Railroad. It was the cattle shipping point for all of West Texas in the early 1880s. There are a few historic homes and buildings in Colorado City.

For more information

You can make reservations or get more information by writing the Superintendent, Lake Colorado City State Recreation Area, Rt. 2, Box 232, Colorado City, TX 79512. The phone number is (915) 728-3931.

Other places to see

Big Spring is 32 miles to the west. The Diamond M Museum in Snyder has one of the finest private art collections in the West. It was assembled by rancher C.T. McLaughlin. He was one of the big beneficiaries of the Scurry County oil boom. McLaughlin died in 1974. His art museum is in the Diamond M Building at 909 25th Street in Snyder, 30 miles north on State Highway 208.

Left: Lakes are a relatively recent phenomenon in West Texas. West Texans make heavy use of resorts like the Lake Colorado City State Recreation Area.

Opposite: The main features of the Big Spring State Recreation Area are the scenic drive and overlook. The park is on top of a small mountain immediately south of Big Spring. The stone shelter was built by the CCC in the 1930s. There is a playground adjacent to it.

BIG SPRING STATE RECREATION AREA

On F.M. 700 on the south side of Big Spring in Howard County.
Entrance fee: $1 per car

This small park is on a mesa on top of Big Spring Mountain overlooking the city of Big Spring and a lot of countryside, too. The park is 344 acres. It was a city park until Big Spring gave it to the State Parks Board in 1934. The CCC came in then and made some improvements. One of the improvements was a dance pavillion. The parks built in the 1930s all had dance terraces or dance pavillions. The pavillion the CCC men built is still here, but it is now called a shade pavillion. Nobody dances in pavillions anymore, but they made a lot of sense before air conditioning.

There is no campground here. The main features in this park are a scenic drive, a lookout point on the edge of the mesa, a nature trail and 14 picnic tables near the shade pavillion. There is also a prairie dog town. Many of the parks in this part of the state have colonies of prairie dogs because people like to watch the little creatures.

For more information

There is nothing here to be reserved, but you can get more information if you need it by writing to the Superintendent, Big Spring State Recreation Area, Box 1064, Big Spring, TX 79721. The phone number is (915) 263-4931.

Other places to see

The Heritage Museum at 510 Scurry Street in Big Spring has a collection of pioneer artifacts, antiques, old photographs and Western art. The old Potton house at 200 Gregg is open to visitors.

MACKENZIE STATE RECREATION AREA

On U.S. 87 and U.S. 82 in Lubbock in Lubbock County. No entrance fee

This park covers 549 acres near downtown Lubbock. It is nothing like most people expect West Texas to be. The park is in Yellowhouse Canyon, where the Yellowhouse Draw and Blackwater Draw meet to form the Double Mountain Fork of the Brazos River. There is water and there are trees. The city of Lubbock is developing a series of lakes along Yellowhouse and Blackwater. The plan is to create one of the biggest urban parks in America. Mackenzie Park will be just a small unit of that park. Much of the land in these draws is unsuitable for anything except park use because it is subject to flash flooding. This part of the state does not get a lot of rain, but the rains sometimes come all at once.

Mackenzie Park was named for Col. Ranald Mackenzie of the U.S. Army. He made this part of Texas habitable when he forced the Comanche Indians out in a military campaign that ended in Palo Duro Canyon in September, 1874.

The park was established originally by the city of Lubbock. The city gave it to the Texas Parks Board in 1938. The Parks Board leased it back to the city in 1958. The city has maintained and operated it ever since. The CCC built some of the improvements, including a golf course and the inevitable dance terrace.

This park also has a prairie dog colony. The prairie dog is a kind of ground squirrel. Prairie dogs live in burrows. The burrows are connected by underground tunnels. Prairie dog communities are made up of families and the families are very conscious of their turf. A prairie dog entering the wrong burrow is made to feel most unwelcome. Prairie dogs pursuing their lifestyle can entertain children as well as any Disney cartoon. Disney may have gotten some of his ideas from prairie dogs.

Mackenzie Park has 56 individual picnic sites. The golf course is managed by the city. Greens fees are $5.50 on weekdays and $7 on weekends.

For more information

You can get more information about the Mackenzie State Recreation Area from the Parks Department, City Hall, Lubbock, TX 79408. The phone number is (806) 762-6411.

Other places to see

Lubbock has one of the outstanding museums in the state. The Museum of Texas Tech University includes the Ranching Heritage Center. This is a collection of historic ranch homes, ranch buildings and ranch equipment gathered from all over Texas. The exhibits are arranged in natural settings and screened from the rest of the Tech campus; so visitors can almost feel they are in the Old West. A visit to the Ranching Heritage Center is a must.

Top: One of the authentic old ranch buildings in the Ranching Heritage Center in the Museum of Texas Tech, Lubbock.

Opposite: Picnic sites surround the small lake in MacKenzie State Recreation Area near downtown Lubbock.

PALO DURO CANYON STATE PARK

On State Highway 217, 12 miles east of Canyon in Randall County.
Entrance fee: $2 per car

Wind and water carved Palo Duro Canyon over a period of hundreds of millions of years. The level High Plains stretch farther than the eye can see to the north and west and south of the city of Canyon. The vista breaks suddenly here east of the city. The drop down to the canyon floor is 800 feet. The canyon is very narrow at the upper end, then widens gradually. The walls get farther apart and the floor spreads and blends in with the Rolling Plains. People in this part of Texas refer to the boundary between the Rolling Plains and the High Plains as the Cap Rock. The boundary is everywhere marked by abrupt cliffs. They are nowhere else as spectacular as they are here.

The Palo Duro Creek rises about 70 miles west of here in Deaf Smith County. It joins the Prairie Dog Town Fork of the Red River at Canyon. This stream is responsible for this awesome gash in the High Plains. Geologists say they can identify sedimentary layers going back 300 million years in the faces of the cliffs exposed by the erosion here. Archaeologists say there is evidence that primitive people hunted mammoths here during the Ice Age.

The climate in the canyon is more benign than that on the High Plains. Many tribes were here before them, but the Comanches were the last native Americans to live here. It was their Shangri-La. The Comanches came down from the Northern Plains around 1700 and discovered the horses the Spanish had brought to the New World. The Comanches were buffalo hunters. Nobody needed horses worse than they did and nobody mastered horsemanship the way they did. A few thousand Comanches controlled the High Plains for more than 150 years. They followed the buffalo wherever the buffalo went. They raided Anglo settlements in Central Texas and Mexican settlements south of the Rio Grande. The Comanche problem was one reason the Spanish agreed to let Anglos settle in Texas. One of the things the Mexicans asked in the treaty that ended the Mexican War was that the United States take responsibility for keeping the Comanches out of Mexico. The Comanches spent their time between their raids and their buffalo hunts in camps on the floor of this canyon.

Col. Ranald Mackenzie learned about the Comanche hide-out from a Mexican trader his troops captured. Mackenzie made a surprise raid into the canyon in September, 1874. The Comanches scattered, but Mackenzie's troops were able

View of the canyon from the Palo Duro State Park interpretative center on the canyon rim near the park entrance. Spanish explorers gave this canyon its name. Palo Duro is Spanish for hard wood.

to separate them from their horses. The Indians spent the winter on the plains without horses and decided to give up. They agreed to move to a reservation in the Oklahoma Territory. They had brought some of their problems upon themselves, but the record on the other side included duplicity and broken promises too. The Comanches' departure opened the plains to settlers. The first ranch in the Panhandle was established by John Goodnight in 1876 near the head of Palo Duro Canyon.

The State Parks Board bought 15,000 acres for a park here in 1933. The Parks Board had no money to spend on parks at the time; so the board arranged to pay Fred and Millie Emery $377,000 in installments out of revenues from the operation of the park.

The board levied an entrance fee of 35 cents and granted some concessions. The board claimed a percentage of the revenue from the concessions and eventually paid for the park. It has been a good investment.

The entrance to Palo Duro Canyon State Park is at the north end of the canyon at the High Plains level. There is an interpretive center and scenic overlook on the rim of the canyon. The park road dives down into the canyon after it passes the center and overlook. You will cross the Prairie Dog Town Fork of the Red River six times on this road before you reach the scenic overlook at the south end of the park. This park road is the only access to the six camping areas in the park. It also goes by the Pioneer Amphitheater, where the Texas Panhandle Heritage Foundation presents the historical pageant *Texas* on summer evenings.

A concessionaire runs a stable near the amphitheater. He rents horses by the hour and can arrange trail rides for groups. Another concessionaire in the canyon offers rides around some of the scenic spots on a miniature train. But camping and hiking are the big attractions here.

The park has 43 tent campsites for $4 a night. There are 51 sites with water and electricity for $6 and 20 sites with water, electricity and sewer connections for $7 a night. Four of the eight restrooms in the park have showers. There are also 96 picnic sites, a trading post, a hiking trail and a replica of the crude dugout John Goodnight lived in when he was starting his ranch here.

For more information

You can make reservations or get more information about this park by writing to the Superintendent, Rt. 2, Box 285, Canyon, TX 79015. The phone number is (806) 488-2227. The number for the amphitheater is (806) 655-2181.

Other places to see

The Panhandle-Plains Museum in Canyon is one of the better museums in the state. The city of Amarillo is just 23 miles north of the park. The Alibates Flint Quarry off State Highway 136, 30 miles north of Amarillo, supplied material for arrowheads and spearpoints for generations of Indians. It is a national monument now and there is still plenty of flint.

Tickets for the historic drama *Texas* are $5, $6 and $7 for adults; $2.50, $3 and $7 for children under 12.

CAPROCK CANYONS STATE PARK

State Highway 86, 3½ miles north of Quitaque in Briscoe County.
Entrance fee: $2 per car

This park was a ranch for almost 100 years before the Parks and Wildlife Department bought it in 1973. It was part of the Comanches' domain until 1874. This is the edge of the Cap Rock escarpment that separates the High Plains from the Rolling Plains. The Comanches' hide-out was north of here in the upper Palo Duro Canyon. The Indians passed this way when they were going south to raid settlements. They came back this way with the horses and cattle they stole from the settlers.

The Indians made a regular practice of swapping stolen livestock for guns and ammunition, whiskey and anything else they needed. One of the places where they did their swapping was near here. The traders supplying the Comanches' needs were known as Comancheros. They hauled their merchandise here from New Mexico. They drove the livestock they acquired back to New Mexico and sold it. They were not popular. Everybody knew they knew the livestock had been stolen.

A Comanchero named Jose Tafoya had a camp near the town of Quitaque. He often had big herds of horses on hand. The name of the place apparently comes from that time. *Quitaque* is supposed to be an Indian word for horse manure. Jose Tafoya played an unintentional role in the Comanches' downfall. Col. Ranald Mackenzie's troops captured Tafoya in 1874 and forced him to reveal the location of the Indians' canyon hide-out.

The first rancher to claim the land that is now the park was George Baker. He sold out to the J.A. Ranch in 1880 and the land changed hands several more times before Theo Geisler bought it in 1936. Geisler ran cattle here until he died in 1969. The small lake he built is still called Lake Theo. This is one of the biggest state parks. It covers 13,000 acres. It opened in 1982.

The North and South Prongs of the Little Red River meet here in the park and there is an abundance of wildlife and birds. Geisler brought in some aoudad sheep from Africa in 1957. They and the native mule deer, coyotes, bobcats and raccoons enjoy the security that goes with living in a state park. The cottonwood, mesquite, hackberry and juniper trees in the canyons provide plenty of cover. The little lake is stocked. There is a fishing pier and a boat ramp. Only small boats are allowed. There is a speed limit of 15 miles an hour. Part of the lake is reserved for swimming.

The park has 14 miles of trails and bridle paths. A tent camping area is reserved for campers with horses. It has a corral, a windmill and a parking area for horse trailers. The camping fee is $4 a night. There are 40 primitive and tent campsites

Caprock Canyons State Park occupies part of what was Comanche country until the 1870s. Daytime temperatures here are often above 100 degrees in the summer. The most pleasant times are spring and fall. The small lake in this park is stocked with crappie, sunfish, largemouth bass and channel catfish.

on the trails and the fee for these is also $4 a night. There is no water in the primitive and tent camping areas and no campfires are allowed. Campers should bring portable stoves and fuel.

The park has 10 campsites with water, table and grill for $4 a night and 25 sites with water, electricity, table and grill for $6 a night in the main camping area near the lake. These campsites and the 40 individual picnic sites in the park all have shade shelters. The restrooms in the main camping area have showers. There is one group picnic shelter with eight tables. It will accommodate up to 50 people. The fee for the group shelter is $8 a day for groups up to 25 and $16 a day for groups of more than 25.

For more information

The address for reservations or further information is Park Superintendent, Caprock Canyons State Park, Box 204, Quitaque, TX 79255. The phone number is (806) 455-1492.

Other places to see

Anglers may want to try a bigger lake. Mackenzie Reservoir, off State Highway 207 about 40 miles northwest, is stocked with large-mouth and small-mouth bass and walleyes. The late country music star Bob Wills grew up at Turkey, 17 miles east of Caprock Canyons State Park. The town has a small monument to him. Wills wrote "San Antonio Rose."

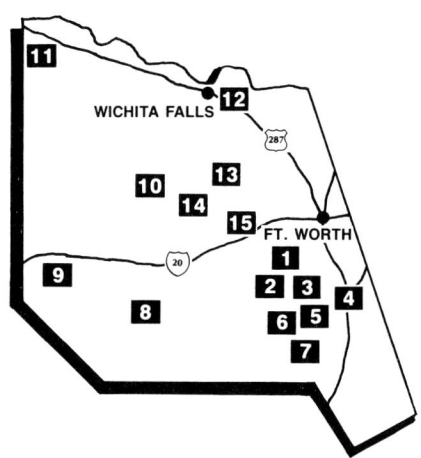

1. Acton State Historic Site
2. Dinosaur Valley State Park
3. Cleburne State Recreation Area
4. Jeff Davis State Recreation Area
5. Lake Whitney State Recreation Area
6. Meridian State Recreation Area
7. Mother Neff State Park
8. Lake Brownwood State Recreation Area
9. Abilene State Recreation Area
10. Fort Griffin State Historical Park
11. Copper Breaks State Park
12. Lake Arrowhead State Recreation Area
13. Fort Richardson State Historical Park
14. Possum Kingdom State Recreation Area
15. Lake Mineral Wells State Park

REGION II
PARKS IN NORTH CENTRAL TEXAS

Nine of the 15 state parks in North Central Texas are within 75 miles of Fort Worth. The Parks and Wildlife Department is developing a large new park even closer to Fort Worth.

Fort Worth is the principal city in this area. The parks in the area are numbered as you would come to them traveling south from Fort Worth and then going clockwise. The parks are not ranked according to their merit because some people are looking for one thing in a park and some are looking for another. I believe the park in this area with the most pluses is Lake Whitney. Cleburne and Meridian are both very attractive, but they have less water. Possum Kingdom has plenty of water. You may prefer it to Lake Whitney. People interested in geology and archaeology may prefer Dinosaur Valley. History buffs may prefer Fort Richardson or Fort Griffin.

Parks Under Development

There is one state park under development in this region. The tentative name is Eagle Mountain Lake Park. The site is on the eastern shore of Eagle Mountain Lake, off F.M. 1220 northwest of Fort Worth. It is approximately 400 acres. The Parks and Wildlife Department paid about $4 million for it in 1980.

ACTON STATE HISTORIC SITE

2½ miles south of U.S. 377 (take F.M. 208 south from 377, go 2 miles into Acton, turn left at Exxon station onto F.M. 1190 and go ½ mile to gate of Acton Cemetery on the right). There is a Parks and Wildlife Department sign at the gate, but no signs marking the route. In Hood County, 35 miles southwest of Fort Worth. No fee

This is the smallest park in the state system. The Parks and Wildlife Department maintains just the Crockett family plot in this old graveyard. Davy Crockett's widow is buried here. Crockett's first wife had died years earlier. He left his second wife at home in Tennessee when he came to Texas in 1836 to join William Barret Travis's little garrison at the Alamo. Crockett was killed by the Mexicans there on March 6. This made his heirs eligible for a land grant, but Mrs. Elizabeth Crockett did not come to Texas to claim the grant until 1853. The choice land was all claimed by then. Mrs. Crockett had to give a surveyor half of her land for locating a tract she could claim.

The land Mrs. Crockett claimed was in northeast Hood County, a few miles from the community of Acton. This is the oldest settlement in Hood County, but no railroad ever came this way and Acton almost disappeared until the development of Lake Granbury revived it.

Other places to see

Other places you may want to see in this area are Granbury (where the courthouse and the entire square surrounding it are listed in the National Register of Historic Places); Dinosaur Valley State Park, 27 miles south off F.M. 205, 5½ miles west of Glen Rose; and Cleburne State Recreation Area, 42 miles southeast on Park Road 21 off U.S. 67 between Glen Rose and Cleburne. Dinosaur Valley and Cleburne both have campgrounds.

Left: The state does not own this site. But the legislature appropriated the money to build the monument and the Parks and Wildlife Department maintains the Crockett cemetery plot as a park.

Opposite: Bill Wylie of the Parks and Wildlife Department staff designed this imaginative new headquarters building for the Dinosaur Valley State Park.

DINOSAUR VALLEY STATE PARK

Off F.M. 205, 5½ miles west of Glen Rose on the Paluxy River in Somervell County, 60 miles southwest of Fort Worth. Entrance fee: $2 per car

This part of Texas was a vast coastal swamp millions of years ago. Dinosaurs lived here. There are not many places where the evidence is as dramatic as the evidence here. The dinosaur tracks here are real, but the two great reptiles on display here are not. They were made of fiberglass in 1964 for the Sinclair Oil Company exhibit at the New York World's Fair. The Sinclair Company's advertising was tied to a dinosaur theme for many years. The Atlantic Richfield Company dropped the theme when it bought out Sinclair. These life-size dinosaur models became surplus about the time the state of Texas was acquiring this site. Atlantic Richfield donated them in 1970.

The tracks were made a hundred million years ago by monsters known today as Pleurocelus and Acrocanthosaurus. The Pleurocelus grew to a length of 70 feet and lived on vegetation. The Acrocanthosaurus was a meat-eater and grew to a height of around 15 feet. The ground was soft when the dinosaurs lived here and the big reptiles left deep footprints where they walked. The soft ground hardened into rock over the centuries and the footprints filled in. The land rose and sank perhaps several times. The climate changed. The Paluxy River developed and eventually the river washed the dirt out of the hardened footprints leaving some of them exposed.

Two brothers named Charlie and William Moss reported the footprints in 1912. Scientists and curiosity seekers came to look. Some of the footprints were cut out of the rock and hauled off to the Museum of Natural History in New York and the Texas Memorial Museum in Austin to be put on display. Some were cut out and sold.

Some local citizens got an option in the early 1960s on 350 acres of land including some of the surviving footprints. They started promoting the idea of a state park. The legislature about the same time authorized the state to start charging fees

for admission to state parks. This legislation also authorized the sale of bonds to raise money for more parks and park improvements. The Parks and Wildlife Department bought this land in 1969 and opened the park the next year.

The park covers 1,270 acres on both sides of the Paluxy River. There are five miles of hiking trails and seven primitive camping areas along these trails. Part of the state's herd of longhorn cattle lives here. The longhorns and the primitive camping areas are across the river from the main part of the park. The river bottom is rocky and the water level is seldom high. It is possible to walk across the river most of the time. There is an interpretive center near the fiberglass dinosaurs where visitors can learn more about dinosaurs and the geology of this area. A group picnic pavillion that can accommodate up to 30 people is available for no extra charge. There is a swimming hole in the river near the pavillion.

The park has six tent camping sites with water for $4 a night and 40 sites with water and electricity for $6 a night. The primitive campsites across the river have no water. They are $4 a night.

Signs direct visitors to the dinosaur tracks; so there is no danger you will miss them unless you are handicapped. The Parks and Wildlife Department has made a major effort to make its attractions accessible to the handicapped. But the dinosaur tracks are in the riverbed. It is necessary to climb down a fairly steep trail to reach the riverbed. People on crutches or in wheelchairs cannot negotiate this trail.

This is limestone and cedar country. The trees are not tall; so the campsites do not have much shade.

For more information

You can make reservations or get more information on the Dinosaur Valley State Park by writing the Superintendent, Box 396, Glen Rose, TX 76043 or by calling (817) 897-4588.

Other places to see

The town of Glen Rose offers a small museum on the square with some history of the dinosaur tracks. Also nearby are Cleburne State Recreation Area, 17 miles east on Park Road 21 off U.S. 67; Lake Whitney State Recreation Area, 50 miles southwest off F.M. 1244, 4 miles southwest of Whitney; and Meridian State Recreation Area, 28 miles south on State Highway 22, 4 miles southwest of Meridian. Cleburne, Lake Whitney and Meridian all have good campgrounds.

Left: Two fiberglass dinosaurs were retired to the Dinosaur Valley State Park after the New York World's Fair.

Opposite: Central Texans have been enjoying the Cleburne State Recreation Area for 50 years. Cedar Lake is the main attraction.

CLEBURNE STATE RECREATION AREA

Off Park Road 21 south of U.S. 67, 12 miles southwest of Cleburne in Johnson County, 43 miles south of Fort Worth. Entrance fee: $2 per car

This is the state campground nearest Six Flags and many campers come here for this reason. This is one of our older parks. Some local businessmen bought the land in 1934 and turned it over to the State Parks Board so it could be developed under the arrangement the board had with the CCC and the National Park Service.

This is limestone and cedar country, but there are oak and elm trees here, too. There have been springs here as long as anyone can remember. The Comanche Indians supposedly used this little valley as one of their stopping points when they were coming down from the Panhandle to raid the pioneer settlements before the Civil War.

The CCC built a dam to capture the water from the springs. The Corps also built a bathhouse, shelter and a residence for the park superintendent. The residence is still here. The original bathhouse and shelter burned a number of years ago. They have been replaced. The park covers 529 acres. The lake is only 116 acres; so no large boats are allowed. It is a lake for small sailboats, canoes and

pedal boats. The park store has canoes and pedal boats for rent and also sells fishing bait, snacks and camping supplies. There is a fishing pier and boat ramp. The fish caught here are mostly crappie.

The park has a mini-bike trail, two playgrounds and a nature trail. Deer, raccoon and quail might be spotted in the woods year-round. The park is usually at its best in the spring when many species of birds visit and the bluebonnets are in bloom. I think the smell of the cedar is refreshing in every season, here and at the Meridian park, too.

There are 40 individual picnic sites. There is one group shelter available at $50 a night. The park has six screened shelters in the woods on the lake shore for rent at $8 a night. There are 27 campsites with water, electricity and sewer connections at $7 a night and 31 sites with water and electricity at $6 a night.

For more information

You can write to the Superintendent, Rt. 2, Box 90, Cleburne, TX 76031 for reservations or more information about Cleburne State Recreation Area, or you can call (817) 645-4215.

Other places to see

Some other places you may be interested in visiting in this area are Dinosaur Valley State Park, 17 miles west off F.M. 205, 5½ miles west of Glen Rose; Meridian State Recreation Area, 45 miles south off State Highway 22, 4 miles southwest of Meridian; and Lake Whitney State Recreation Area, 48 miles southeast off F.M. 1244, 4 miles southwest of Whitney. Dinosaur Valley, Meridian and Lake Whitney all have good campgrounds.

JEFF DAVIS STATE RECREATION AREA

On unpaved road, south of State Highway 22, just east of I-35 on eastern outskirts of Hillsboro in Hill County, 51 miles south of Fort Worth. No fee

This is not one of the Parks and Wildlife Department's showplaces. I have included it only because it is listed with the state parks. You do not want to come here.

This is an old reunion ground deeded to the State Parks Board in 1924 by the Confederate Veterans and Old Settlers Association of Hill County. The Parks Board turned it over to an American Legion Post in Hillsboro. It is 37 acres surrounding a small arena that is used once a year by a rodeo association. The grounds are grown up in weeds. There is no campground, no picnic tables and no staff. But there are people in Hill County with pleasant memories of reunions here in earlier times.

Confederate veterans and old Hill County settlers used to have big reunions here. Interest in reunions waned. The veterans and settlers deeded the site to the state. The state leased it to an American Legion post and the legionnaires leased it to the Hill County Roundup Club. It is not easy to say who is most to blame for the poor condition of the property.

LAKE WHITNEY STATE RECREATION AREA

Off F.M. 1244, 4 miles southwest of Whitney in Hill County, 74 miles south of Fort Worth. Entrance fee: $2 per vehicle or plane

The Texas Parks and Wildlife Department has something for almost everybody and here is the proof. Some Texans like to do their traveling in their own planes. Not every resort can accommodate them. Lake Whitney State Recreation Area can. This park has an airstrip. Some campers fly in. They are treated the same as the motoring folks. They pay $2 per plane plus the fee for whatever camping site they use.

The Army engineers created Lake Whitney when they built a dam across the Brazos in 1951 just southwest of the town of Whitney. The purpose of the dam is to control flooding and generate power, but the lake has generated a lot of recreational opportunities, too. Lake Whitney is 45 miles long. Parks and resorts are scattered along both banks. This park is on the east shore of the lake at its widest point.

The park is just under 1,000 acres. Some of it is wooded. Much of it is open and filled with wildflowers in the spring. There is not much to draw divers here, but the opportunities for all other watersports are present. There is plenty of protected water for skiing. Fishermen get striped bass, black bass, white bass, crappie and catfish here. The park has a boat ramp, fish-cleaning tables, a hiking trail and a mini-bike trail.

Lake Whitney Recreation Area is popular with campers and with people just looking for a pleasant place to spend the day. A large picnic area overlooks the swimming beach in the park. A recreation hall, a group shelter and 137 campsites are laid out around the waterfront.

The recreation hall can accommodate up to 100 people for meals and it rents for $40 a day. The hall can also be rented overnight for $70. It can sleep 30 people. A group camp with a dining hall and eight screened shelters rents for $50 plus $8 for each shelter required. Utensils and linens are not provided.

The park has 95 individual tent campsites with water for $4 a night. There are seven sites with water and electricity for $6 a night and 35 sites with water, electricity and sewer connections for $7 a night. There are 48 screened shelters for rent at $8 a night. The park is a favorite with many veteran campers.

For more information

You can make reservations or get more information about Lake Whitney State Recreation Area by writing to the Superintendent, Box 1175, Whitney, TX 76692 or by calling (817) 694-3793.

Other places to see

You may also want to visit several parks maintained by the Corps of Engineers around the lake and Hillsboro (Confederate Research Center and Museum at Hill County College and one of the great Texas courthouses). There is a campground at Meridian State Recreation Area, 34 miles southwest off State Highway 22, 4 miles southwest of Meridian.

Top: Lake Whitney State Recreation Area is a popular place for family reunions. The Corps of Engineers also maintains about a dozen small parks around this lake.

Right: Most of the campers at Lake Whitney State Recreation Area come in cars. A few fly in. The park has a landing strip and plenty of parking space for the campers' planes.

MERIDIAN STATE RECREATION AREA

Off State Highway 22, 4 miles southwest of Meridian in Bosque County, 70 miles southwest of Fort Worth. Entrance fee: $2 per car

This park was established during the Depression and developed by the CCC. It has the standard CCC trademarks: a small lake, a stone building and terrace. Other improvements have been added since the 1930s and these were modernized in 1967. It is not near a main highway; so not a lot of people know what a pleasant spot it is.

The park is not large. It is just over 500 acres. Most of the land was donated in 1933 and 1934. The dam the men of the CCC built across Bee Creek impounds a lake that covers about 70 acres in wet years. The lake shrinks substantially during the frequent dry periods.

The area is full of limestone and juniper. The tree most Texans call cedar is really the Ashe juniper. Several varieties of oak grow here, too, along with yucca, mountain laurel and prickly pear cactus. Much of the park is wooded, but there are some open areas and these areas are filled with bluebonnets and other wildflowers in the spring. There are deer, raccoons and possums here. Golden-cheeked warblers, ladder-backed woodpeckers, black-capped vireos and canyon wrens make up part of the resident bird population. Several species of waterfowl winter here.

It is difficult to say what a typical Texas location is because of the great variety of the Texas landscape. But I always feel I am truly in Texas when I can see limestone hills, smell juniper and hear the song of the cicadas. Meridian is that kind of place. Cleburne is, too, but this park has more hills than Cleburne.

The lake here is not big enough for skiing. Only canoes and small boats are allowed. Part of the lake is reserved for swimming, but there are no lifeguards. Fishermen get bass, sunfish, crappie and catfish here. A hiking trail goes around the lake. One of the two nature trails is designed especially for young people.

This park has 24 individual picnic sites. A group camp with a large dining hall and seven shelters on the lake shore rents for $106 a night. There are 11 other screened shelters for rent at $8 a night; eight camping sites with water, electrici-

Opposite: Some of the best architects in the country were out of work in the 1930s. Some of them were enlisted to design buildings like this for the state parks. They designed them to last.

ty, sewer connections, table and grill at $7 a night; seven sites with water, electricity, table and grill at $6 a night; and 15 sites with water, table and grill at at $4 a night. Some of the screened shelters are right on the water.

For more information

You can make reservations or get more information about the Meridian State Recreation Area by writing to the Superintendent, Box 188, Meridian, TX 76665 or by calling (817) 435-2536.

Other places to see

Other state parks in this area are Lake Whitney State Recreation Area, 34 miles northeast off F.M. 1244, 4 miles southwest of Whitney; Cleburne State Recreation Area, 45 miles north on Park Road 21 off U.S. 67 between Cleburne and Glen Rose; and Dinosaur Valley State Park, 28 miles north off F.M. 205, 5½ miles west of Glen Rose. All have good campgrounds.

The old Chisholm Trail the South Texas cattlemen followed when they drove their cattle to market in Kansas came through Bosque County a few miles east of the Meridian State Recreation Area. The great Texas folklorist, John Avery Lomax, grew up on a farm outside Meridian. His exposure here to the trail drivers and the cowboys, their stories and songs started him on his life's work.

MOTHER NEFF STATE PARK

Off State Highway 236, 6 miles west of Moody in Coryell County, 128 miles south of Fort Worth.
Entrance fee: $2 per car

Mother Neff is often called Texas' original state park. The first portion was donated to the state in a will Mrs. Isabella Neff wrote in 1916. The state acquired the original six acres here when that will was probated in 1921. Mrs. Neff specified that the land was to be used for religious, educational, fraternal and political purposes. The first improvements here were made by the Neff family and by the religious groups using the park.

Isabella Neff was Pat Neff's mother. She and her husband, Noah, came here from Virginia in 1855. Pat Neff was born near here. He had just been elected governor when his mother died. At the beginning of his second term in 1923, Gov. Neff recommended to the legislature that a State Parks Board be established. He said his mother's gift gave him the idea.

The CCC and the National Park Service started helping the states develop and improve parks in 1933. Pat Neff was president of Baylor University and a member of the Parks Board then. He donated 250 acres of land adjacent to the six acres his mother had donated and the Mother Neff State Park qualified for the CCC improvement program. A stone tabernacle the CCC built then is still in use.

The park now covers 259 acres. About 50 acres is Leon River bottom land. Half of the remainder is limestone hills with juniper and oak. The other half is prairie. One of the trees in this park is the biggest Texas oak in the country.

A shallow cave under a limestone ledge here was once an Indian shelter and burying ground. The military road connecting Austin and Fort Gates at Gatesville ran through here in the 1850s. An old milestone from those days stands near the park headquarters building.

There is no fishing pier, no fish-cleaning table and no boat ramp, but some visitors do fish from the river bank. There is a hiking trail and a playground. A group shelter that will accommodate up to 175 people rents for $8 a day for small groups and $16 a day for groups of more than 26. The rock tabernacle is available for groups of up to 200 at the same rates.

The 15 campsites here with water, table and grill rent for $4 a night. There are six sites with water, electricity, table and grill for $6 a night. The restrooms have hot showers. There is a sanitary dump station.

For more information

The address for reservations or more information about Mother Neff State Park is Rt. 1, Box 58, Moody, TX 76557. The phone number is (817) 853-2389.

Other places to see

Other places close by are Waco, 33 miles northeast; Texas Ranger Museum at Fort Fisher on I-35 at Riverside and the Browning Library on the Baylor University campus at South 8th and Speight Street; and Fort Hood, 43 miles southwest, main gate on U.S. 190 just west of Killeen (open to visitors, two military museums).

About one-fourth of the area of Mother Neff State Park is heavily wooded bottom land along the Leon River.

LAKE BROWNWOOD STATE RECREATION AREA

Off State Highway 279, 22 miles northwest of Brownwood in Brown County, 118 miles southwest of Fort Worth. Entrance fee: $2 per car

The Brown County Water Control and Improvement District No. 1 created Lake Brownwood by damming Pecan Bayou to get water for Brownwood. The water district deeded 538 acres of land on the lake shore to the State Parks Board in 1933. The CCC did the original development.

The lake and the park were named for the city of Brownwood. Brownwood and Brown County were named after Henry Brown. He came to Texas in 1824. He lived in Brazoria, Gonzales and San Antonio. He was a noted Indian fighter and opponent of Mexican rule. Brown died in 1834, 22 years before this county was created.

Lake Brownwood covers 7,300 acres; so there is room for all water sports and no limit on boat or motor size. There are boat ramps and docks, a lighted fishing pier, fish-cleaning tables and a park store. The swimming beach has no lifeguards. There are hiking trails, a nature trail and a mini-bike trail.

The original CCC improvements here included the usual stone clubhouse and dance terrace on the lake shore. The park has 17 cabins overlooking the lake. They rent at $18 a night for one or two people, plus $4 for each additional adult and $1 for each additional child. Children under 6 are free.

There are 14 campsites with water, table and grill for $4 a night; 55 sites with water, electricity, table and grill for $6 a night; and 20 sites with water, electricity, sewer connections, table and grill for $7 a night. There are 10 screened shelters for $8 a night.

This park is unusually well provided with places for group events. There is a group dining hall with five bunk houses nearby. The dining hall rents for $50 and the bunk houses are $8 each. Groups up to 32 can meet here.

The Beach Lodge, on the waterfront, rents for $80. It can sleep up to 26 people. Fisherman Lodge is smaller and farther from the water. It sleeps up to 10

Left: The men of the Civilian Conservation Corps did some of their better work here at Lake Brownwood State Recreation Area. This shelter overlooks the lake. It was built in the 1930s.

Opposite: The individual cabins the CCC built in the 1930s were modernized in the 1970s. They are as comfortable as any in the state park system.

people and rents for $50 a night. The dining hall and lodges have kitchens and restrooms. Towels and linens are furnished. Utensils and dishes are not. The same is true of the cabins.

Fishing is the big attraction here. Most of the fish caught are crappie, bass and catfish.

For more information

You can make reservations or get more information about Lake Brownwood State Recreation Area by writing to the Superintendent, Rt. 5, Box 160, Brownwood, TX 76801 or by calling (915) 784-5223.

Other places to see

Howard Payne College and the Douglas MacArthur Academy of Freedom are nearby in the city of Brownwood. The 36th Division Memorial Park is located on what was part of Camp Bowie. The original Camp Bowie was in Tarrant County during World War I. The 36th Division trained for World War II at the second Camp Bowie here outside Brownwood. Most of what was the base is now an industrial park.

A good part of the Texas pecan crop is grown in this area.

ABILENE STATE RECREATION AREA

Off F.M. 89, 19 miles southwest of Abilene in Taylor County, 162 miles southwest of Fort Worth.
Entrance fee: $2 per car

The groves of pecan trees in this park sheltered Indian camps periodically until the 1870s. This was a popular place with the Tonkawas and later with the Comanches because the buffalo came through here on their north and south migrations. The row of hills here is called the Callahan Divide. The only break in the hills is five miles northeast of the park. This natural pass has been called Buffalo Gap for more than a hundred years because the buffalo sensibly traveled through it instead of climbing up and down the hills. The best source of water here then was Elm Creek. The Indian buffalo hunters and, later, the white buffalo hunters camped along Elm Creek. This park is on Elm Creek; so it is a place that has seen a lot of coming and going since long before Winnebagos.

The city of Abilene put a dam across Elm Creek in 1921 to create a water supply for the city. The city gave this land, just below the dam, to the State Parks Board in 1933. The CCC built the original improvements including a swimming pool and a concession building with a dance terrace. The shelters and campgrounds were added in the 1960s and 70s without disturbing the original pecan grove.

The park covers over 600 acres. The swimming pool and the park store are open only during the summer, from Memorial Day through Labor Day. The rest of the park is open year-round. There are eight screened shelters for rent at $8 a night; 12 tent campsites with table and grill at $4 a night; and 35 sites with water, electricity, table and grill at $6 a night. The park has one group area with a dining hall, restrooms and 48 campsites with water and electricity. The fee is $50 for the dining hall and the campsites are $6 each. The dining hall has a stove and refrigerator. Another group mess hall is available for day use only at $50 a day. This building also has a stove, refrigerator, tables, benches and restrooms.

Serious anglers will not be tempted by the little bit of water that is normally in Elm Creek here, but they can and do fish free in the waters of Lake Abilene right across the road.

For more information

The address for inquiries or reservations is Superintendent, Abilene State Recreation Area, Rt. 1, Tuscola, TX 79562. The phone number is (915) 572-3204.

Other places to see

The Butterfield stage road came through the town of Buffalo Gap (about 10 miles north of the park on F.M. 89) for the same reason the buffalo did. Buffalo Gap was the most important town and county seat in this area until the railroad came in the 1880s and created the new town of Abilene. The ruins of old Fort Phantom Hill are on private property on F.M. 600 about 15 miles north of Abilene.

Top: The park store in the Abilene State Recreation Area occupies part of the stone headquarters building the CCC built in 1933. There is a swimming pool next door.

Right: Most of the visitors come in the summer, but the campgrounds in the Abilene State Recreation Area are open the year round.

FORT GRIFFIN STATE HISTORICAL PARK

On U.S. 283, 15 miles north of Albany in Shackelford County, 137 miles west of Fort Worth. Entrance fee: $2 per car

The U.S. Army built several forts in West Texas before the Civil War to protect settlers and travelers. Most of those forts were abandoned during the Civil War. The Indians grew bolder and the frontier moved backward toward the east. Settlers and travelers demanded more protection after the war; so several new forts were built in the 1860s. Fort Griffin was one of these. Four companies of the 6th Cavalry commanded by Lt. Col. Samuel Sturgis established the base here in July, 1867. The post was originally called Camp Wilson. The name was changed to Fort Griffin in February, 1868 after Gen. Charles Griffin died of yellow fever in Galveston. Gen. Griffin was commander of the Union occupation force in Texas.

No battles were fought here. The troops stationed here were occupied mainly with patrol duties and providing escorts for the travelers heading for California. But Fort Griffin was an important base and supply point for the U.S. Army campaign that finally ended the Comanche problem in 1874. That campaign was launched after a band of Indians attacked a military wagon train on the road between here and Fort Richardson in 1871. Gen. William T. Sherman was head of the U.S. Army then. He was on the frontier trying to find out if the Indian problem was as bad as the Texans claimed it was. The raid on the wagon train and the massacre of seven teamsters convinced Gen. Sherman the problem was serious. He had passed over the same road where the massacre occurred just the day before.

Shackelford County gave this land to the State Parks Board in 1936. It was designated a state park in 1938. The buildings were already in ruins. Only a few of them had been built of stone; most were frame. Nothing remains of the settlement called the Flat that grew up outside the fort. The Flat, once the biggest and most important settlement in the area, was a supply point and resort for buffalo hunters and cowhands driving cattle to Dodge City. It attracted shady characters and loose women in large numbers. Bat Masterson, Wyatt Earp and Doc Holliday spent some time at the Flat. The settlement had a population of 1,000 at its peak. The Flat faded away after the Army abandoned the fort in 1881.

This park is divided into two units totaling 506 acres. The ruins of the fort are in one unit on the west side of the U.S. 283. The campgrounds and picnic sites are in the other unit on the east side of the highway. This park is the home base of the state's longhorn herd; so you are sure to see some longhorns wandering around. They are no longer as rare as they were when the state herd was established in the early 1920s. They were close to becoming extinct then.

There is a visitors center at the ruins where visitors can pick up some background on the fort. There is no guided tour, but visitors can walk around the grounds and see what is left. The ruins are marked and identified.

The recreational unit of this park fronts on the Clear Fork of the Brazos River. You can catch a catfish here, but there is no guarantee. The park has a playground and five picnic sites. A group shelter on the river bank rents for $8 a day for groups up to 25 or $16 for groups of more than 25. The park has five campsites with water, table and grill for $4 a night and 15 sites with water and electricity for $6 a night.

The superintendent's residence, beside the entrance to this unit of the park, is an old ranch house built in 1874.

For more information

You can write to the Superintendent, Fort Griffin State Historical Park, Rt. 1, Albany, TX 76430 or phone (915) 762-3592 for reservations or more information about this park.

Other places to see

Also in this area are the town of Albany (an 1880s courthouse and several other historic buildings, historical pageant and celebration called the "Fandangle" every night during the second two weeks of June); the ruins of Fort Phantom Hill, 42 miles southwest on F.M. 600, 15 miles north of Abilene; and Possum Kingdom State Recreation Area, 73 miles east on Park Road 33, 17 miles north of Caddo. Fort Phantom Hill is in ruins and on private property, but accessible. Possum Kingdom State Recreation Area is a full-blown state park with campgrounds and frontage on a big lake.

Descendants of the longhorns the late Frank Dobie rounded up to create the official state herd in the 1920s are living now at Fort Griffin and several other state parks.

COPPER BREAKS STATE PARK

13 miles south of Quanah on State Highway 6 in Hardeman County, 200 miles northwest of Fort Worth.
Entrance fee: $2 per car

The Comanche Indians ruled this part of the world until the early 1870s. The last war chief of the Quahadi branch of the Comanche tribe was Quanah Parker. The town 13 miles north of this park was named for him. Quanah Parker's mother was a white woman the Comanches had kidnapped in 1836. Texas Rangers recaptured Cynthia Ann Parker on the south bank of the Pease River just a few miles east of here in 1860.

The Copper Breaks State Park is on the north bank of the Pease River at the southern end of Hardemann County. It covers almost 1,900 acres. The state bought it in 1970. It was ranch land before that. The visitors center in the park has exhibits, photographs and a slide show detailing some of the history of the area.

Breaks is a word used in this part of the world to describe the broken terrain along rivers and streams. *Breaks* would be canyons most other places. Copper does not occur in commercial quantities, but there is some in the clay in these breaks, hence the name of the park.

There is some juniper in the breaks, but much of this park is grassy mesa. There is a lake, but you won't want to bring your ski boat. The lake covers only 60 acres at the best of times. It is for swimming and fishing. The speed limit is 5 miles an hour. The little lake is stocked with catfish, bass and perch. There is a boat ramp and a small swimming beach, but no lifeguard.

There are 40 picnic tables near the lake, a nature trail, a hiking trail and an amphitheater, where the park staff puts on interpretive programs some summer evenings.

Nature provided very little shade here; so the Parks and Wildlife Department has provided shade shelters at the campsites. There are 25 sites with water, electricity, table and grill on a mesa overlooking the river and the lake at $6 a night. There are 15 campsites without electricity for $4 a night. Insects can be a problem here; so bring your repellant if you come in the summer.

For more information

You can make reservations or get more information about Cooper Breaks State Park by writing to the Superintendent, Rt. 3, Quanah, TX 79252. The phone number is (817) 839-4331.

Other places to see

Other places to see in this neighborhood are not numerous. There is a small museum in the old jail building in Quanah, 13 miles north, and another one in the old jail building in Childress, 43 miles northwest. The Four Sixes (6666) Ranch is 72 miles southwest in the little town of Guthrie on U.S. 83. This big and famous ranch was established by Samuel Burk Burnett and is still owned by his heirs. It was here that some of the early Marlboro Man advertising pictures were made. The ranch is not open to the public, but the main house and the ranch store are right in town. The store is open to the public. There is not another state park within 100 miles of Copper Breaks.

There is little natural shade in Copper Breaks State Park. The Parks and Wildlife Department has built shelters resembling Indian teepees to shade the picnic tables.

LAKE ARROWHEAD STATE RECREATION AREA

On F.M. 1954, 15 miles southeast of Wichita Falls in Clay County, about 100 miles northwest of Fort Worth. Entrance fee: $2 per car

Lake Arrowhead is bigger than most people expect a lake in this part of Texas to be. It is advertised to be 13,500 acres, but it is something less than that during the frequent dry spells. There are no limits on the size of boats or motors. Skiing and fishing are the most popular activities here, but the lake and the park draw birdwatchers and campers, too.

The city of Wichita Falls built Lake Arrowhead in 1965 to improve the city water supply. The Parks and Wildlife Department bought this land from the city in 1970 for $50,000. It is 524 acres and it is at the north end of the lake by the dam. Most of the rivers in Texas flow more or less southward, but several rivers in this part of the state flow northward into the Red River. This lake is on the Little Wichita River. It is one of the streams feeding into the Red; so the dam is on the north end of the lake.

Lake Arrowhead has 106 miles of shore line and much of the shore line outside the park is occupied by private resorts and private homes. Many people keep summer homes here, but some live here year-round. The park and park store are open all year. The store sells food, camping supplies, bait and tackle. It is operated by a concessionaire and is at the boat docks.

The park has a large boat ramp and 43 picnic tables with shade shelters and grills. The picnic area is right on the water. There are 19 campsites with water, table and grill near the shore for $4 a night. The trailer campsites are farther from the water in an area where there are a few mesquite trees. Mesquites don't offer much shade. There are 48 sites in this area with water and electricity for $6 a night. There are parks with more attractive settings, but they are a long way from here. This park seems to be popular; the campground appears well used.

For more information

You can get more information about Lake Arrowhead State Recreation Area or make reservations by writing the Superintendent, Rt. 2, Box 147-A, Wichita Falls, TX 76301 or by calling (817) 528-2211.

Other places to see

The Wichita Mountains Wildlife Refuge is just 60 miles north in Oklahoma if you have a yen to see some of Oklahoma. The nearest Texas state park is Fort Richardson State Historical Park, about 67 miles southeast off U.S. 281. It has a campground.

Some ducks live the year round at Lake Arrowhead. Geese, pelicans and blue herons migrate through here in the fall.

FORT RICHARDSON STATE HISTORICAL PARK

*Off U.S. 281, ½ mile south of Jacksboro in Jack County, 62 miles northwest of Fort Worth.
Entrance fee: $2 per car*

The U.S. Army built this fort in the late 1860s when this was the Indian frontier. The southern road to California came this way in those days. The soldiers stationed here protected the stage coaches and wagon trains and made the settlers feel more secure.

Fort Richardson was established by units of the 6th Calvary in 1866. The fort occupied two other sites briefly before moving to this site in the fall of 1867. The name honors one of the generals killed in the battle of Antietam. Israel B. Richardson was a Union general, of course. The U.S. Army named no forts for Confederate generals.

Col. Ranald Mackenzie was commanding Fort Richardson in the spring of 1871 when a band of Comanche and Kiowa Indians attacked a military wagon train west of here and killed seven teamsters. The head of the U.S. Army was visiting Fort Richardson when a survivor crawled into the post with word of the massacre. Gen. William T. Sherman was touring the frontier to find out if the Indian problems were as bad as he had heard. The general had traveled the very road where the attack occurred just the day before. He gave Col. Mackenzie orders to make war on the Indians and the colonel did little else for the next four years. Four of his campaigns were launched from Fort Richardson. His final victory over the Comanches in Palo Duro Canyon in the fall of 1874 made him one of the Army's most famous Indian fighters.

People made no attempt to save old forts in the nineteenth century. The Fort Richardson buildings were left to the elements when the troops left in 1878. The

frontier had moved farther west. The troops from here went to Fort Griffin in Shackelford County and then moved to Fort Clark when Fort Griffin was abandoned in 1881.

The city of Jacksboro acquired title to the fort eventually and the city deeded it to the Parks and Wildlife Department in 1968. The department bought the adjoining 347 acres in 1970 and 1974 and the park now covers 396 acres.

The biggest buildings at frontier forts usually were the hospitals. The hospital at Fort Richardson was a large stone building with wide verandas. It has been restored and is now a museum with displays illustrating some of the history of the fort and that wagon train raid. Several other buildings have been restored. Some are still in ruins. There is one picnic site with 11 tables near the old fort. Seventeen other picnic sites and the campground are on the other side of Lost Creek. There is also one group site that can accommodate 60 people. It is $8 for groups up to 25 and $16 for larger groups. There is no fee for individual picnic sites in any of the parks.

The park has 15 campsites with water, electricity, table and grill for $6 a night. Some are in deep shade near the creek and some are in semi-shade on higher ground. You may want to ask the ranger to let you drive through to see how the land lies before you choose a site.

A small lake in the old stone quarry has fish in it. Other features include a nature trail, a hiking trail and an old buffalo wallow near the entrance road.

For more information

The address for reservations or more information is Superintendent, Fort Richardson State Historical Park, P.O. Box 4, Jacksboro, TX 76056. The phone number is (817) 567-3506.

Other places to see

Nearby Jacksboro is not a really old town, but it has some interesting nineteenth-century buildings around the square. Lake Mineral Wells State Park is about 34 miles south on U.S. 180, just east of Mineral Wells.

POSSUM KINGDOM STATE RECREATION AREA

On Park Road 33, 17 miles north of Caddo in Palo Pinto County, about 100 miles west of Fort Worth.
Entrance fee: $2 per car

Texas was the first state to delegate to another political entity the authority to build dams, harness rivers and allocate river waters. The first river to get such attention was the Brazos because there had been so many disastrous floods in its watershed. The first river authority was the Brazos River Authority, originally called the Brazos River Reclamation and Conservation District. The first project was the dam that created Possum Kingdom Lake. The WPA put up about half the money.

The Brazos River Reclamation and Conservation District was created by the legislature in 1929. Congress authorized construction of the dam in 1935. It was completed in March, 1941, and named for Morris Sheppard. Sheppard represented Texas in the U.S. House of Representatives for 11 years and then in the Senate for 28 years. He died two weeks after the dam was completed.

The engineers had expected it would take about three years for the lake to fill, but there was a lot of rain in the spring of 1941 and the lake was full a month after the dam was finished. It immediately became a popular fishing resort and still is. Most of the fish caught are black bass, sand bass and catfish.

The Chamber of Commerce at Graham first suggested the idea of a state park on the lake before the dam was finished. The district deeded almost 7,000 acres to the State Parks Board in 1940 with the stipulation that the land be used for a state park. The Parks Board left most of the land undeveloped and the district went to court in 1952 to ask that the acreage be returned because the board had not carried out its end of the bargain. The court gave the biggest part of the land back to the district, but the Parks Board turned what was left into a very respectable park.

The lake covers 20,000 acres and has 310 miles of shore line. The park has about 10 miles of shore line. Some of it is gently sloping and has a swimming beach, but much of the shore line in the park and around the lake is steep cliffs. The limestone cliffs create many quiet coves around the lake. The water is surprisingly clear and many divers and skiers come here.

Part of the official Texas longhorn herd lives in this park along with many deer and, of course, possums. Stories differ on how the name was chosen. One story is that President Roosevelt named the lake because the idea of a possum kingdom caught his fancy. The area was being called the Kingdom of the Possum long before the dam was built.

A few of the old buildings at Fort Richardson have been restored. This was the fort hospital.

There is a picnic area near the swimming beach in this park. The cabins are near the beach, too. There are six cabins with two double beds, kitchen, bath, air conditioning and heating. Every cabin has a fireplace and linens are furnished. The cabin fee is $18 for the first one or two people, $4 for each additional adult and $1 for each additional child. The park has 58 tent campsites with water, table and grill for $4 a night and 58 sites with water, electricity, table and grill for $6 a night. Some of the $6 campsites have shade shelters and some of them are picturesquely perched on cliffs above the lake. Some sites have very little shade.

There is a playground, a boat ramp and a lighted fishing pier. A park store operated by a concessionaire sells food and camping supplies and keeps a fleet of fishing boats for rent. The Brazos River Authority also maintains five recreation areas around the lake with public boat ramps. People come from miles around to watch a fireworks show on the lake every Fourth of July.

People approaching the park from the east, south or west have no trouble finding Park Road 33 at Caddo. People approaching from the north can be confused by highway maps seeming to indicate that F.M. 1148 leads to the park. It does not. But you can take 1148 east from State Highway 67 and then turn south on F.M. 3253. This connects with Park Road 33.

For more information

You can write to the Superintendent, Possum Kingdom State Recreation Area, Box 36, Caddo, TX 76029 or call (817) 549-1803 for reservations or more information about this park.

Other places to see

Nearby places to see are Thurber, 45 miles south on I-20 (a ghost town that once had 20,000 people mining coal and making bricks); Fort Griffin State Historical Park, 73 miles west on U.S. 283 north of Albany; Fort Richardson State Historical Park, 69 miles northeast on U.S. 281 at Jacksboro; and Lake Mineral Wells State Park, 54 miles southeast on U.S 180 just east of Mineral Wells.

Lake Mineral Wells State Park is open year round but the best times to visit here are spring and fall.

LAKE MINERAL WELLS STATE PARK

Off U.S. 180, 4 miles east of Mineral Wells in Parker County, 44 miles west of Fort Worth.
Entrance fee: $2 per car

Most of this park was once part of a big military base called Camp Wolters. It was established in 1926 as a training ground for the National Guard and turned into an infantry training base in World War II. The Army closed the base in 1946. The Air Force took it over in 1951 and changed the name to Wolters Air Force Base. The Army came back in 1956 and started training helicopter pilots here. The name was changed to Fort Wolters. Thousands of helicopter pilots trained here for the Vietnam War. The Army closed the base again in 1974. Some of the property was given or sold to other agencies and concerns. The government gave the state 2,865 acres for this park. The park completely surrounds a lake built to create a water supply for the city of Mineral Wells.

The lake is just 646 acres, but it is big enough for most water sports. There are fishing piers and a boat ramp and the park store has boats for rent as well as camping supplies and food. Hiking trails wind through the fairly rough country around the lake. The park has an equestrian trail and a special parking lot for vehicles towing horse trailers.

There are two campgrounds with restrooms and a total of 28 campsites reserved for backpackers. The campsites are about two miles from the trailhead on the west side of the lake. The equestrian trailhead is nearby. Seventy-eight individual picnic sites are scattered around the southeastern edge of Lake Mineral Wells. There are 30 camp sites with water, table and grill at $4 a night and 80 sites with water, electricity, table and grill at $6 a night on the west side of the lake. There is a trailer dump station and a group camping area with eight screened shelters and a large hall with a kitchen. This camp can be rented for $50 plus $8 for each screened shelter. It can accommodate up to 70 people. This camp has its own restrooms and showers. The shelters have bunk beds, but no bedding or linens are furnished.

For more information

Write to the Superintendent, Rt. 4, Box 39C, Mineral Wells, TX 76067 or phone (817) 328-1171 for reservations or more information about Lake Mineral Wells State Park.

Other places to see

You might like to drive around Mineral Wells while you are here. The town was a thriving health resort and convention center in the days before jet planes and Las Vegas. Two big hotels were built then. One is now vacant; the other is a retirement home. Almost all the mineral baths have closed. The town is still alive, but it is just a town now with no resorts and no military base.

Also in the area are Possum Kingdom State Recreation Area, 54 miles northwest on Park Road 33 north of Caddo; Fort Richardson State Historical Park, 34 miles north on U.S. 281; and Granbury, 45 miles southeast on U.S. 377, where the 1891 courthouse and entire square are listed in the National Register of Historic Places. Possum Kingdom and Fort Richardson both have good campgrounds.

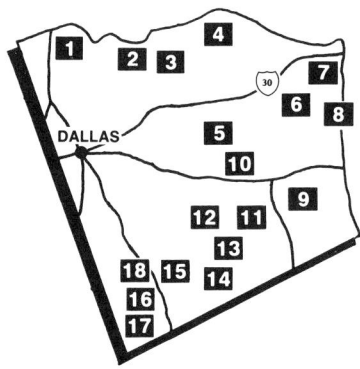

1. Eisenhower State Recreation Area
2. Eisenhower Birthplace State Historic Site
3. Bonham State Recreation Area
4. Sam Bell Maxey House State Historic Structure
5. Governor Hogg Shrine State Historical Park
6. Daingerfield State Park
7. Atlanta State Recreation Area
8. Caddo Lake State Park
9. Martin Creek Lake State Recreation Area
10. Tyler State Park
11. Jim Hogg State Historical Park
12. Rusk-Palestine State Park and Texas State Railroad Historical Park
13. Caddoan Mounds State Historic Site
14. Mission Tejas State Historical Park
15. Fairfield Lake State Recreation Area
16. Fort Parker State Recreation Area
17. Old Fort Parker State Historic Site
18. Confederate Reunion Grounds State Historical Park

REGION III
PARKS IN NORTHEAST TEXAS

The Texas Parks and Wildlife Department maintains 18 parks, recreation areas, historical parks and historic sites in this part of the state. There are six additional parks under development in this area.

The principal city in this section of the state is Dallas. The parks are numbered in this section in the order you would encounter them if you drove north from Dallas to Lake Texoma and then traveled around the area clockwise. The numbers have nothing to do with ranking. My personal favorite is Caddo Lake, but there are several other outstanding parks in this section of the state.

Parks Under Development

There are five parks and one historic structure in the development stage in this section of the state:

Lake Bob Sandlin Park in Titus County on F.M. 21 near Mount Pleasant. The Parks and Wildlife Department has bought about 650 acres since 1979.

Lake Lewisville Park off F.M. 423 near Lewisville in Denton County. Site is 721 acres leased from the Corps of Engineers in 1981.

Lake Tawakoni Park at the end of F.M. 2475 near Tawakoni in Hunt and Rains counties. Site is 401 acres leased from the Sabine River Authority in 1984.

Lakeview Lake Park in the southwestern corner of Dallas County on F.M. 1382 near Cedar Hill on a lake being developed by the Trinity River Authority and the Corps of Engineers. Site is 1,800 acres. The Parks and Wildlife Department bought it in 1982 for about $2.5 million.

Purtis Creek Park on the line between Henderson and Van Zandt counties on F.M. 316 near Eustace. Site is about 1,600 acres, wooded with a small lake. The Parks and Wildlife Department bought the land between 1976 and 1982 for about $2 million.

The historic Starr mansion in Marshall at 407 West Travis was built by James Frank Starr in 1870. Clara Pope Willoughby and Ray Willoughby have donated it to the Parks and Wildlife Department, but it is not yet open to the public.

EISENHOWER STATE RECREATION AREA

7 miles northwest of Denison off F.M. 1310 in Grayson County, 84 miles north of Dallas.
Entrance fee: $2 per car

The Army Engineers created Lake Texoma in 1944 when they completed the Denison Dam to impound the waters of the Washita and Red rivers. The generating plant at the south end of the dam is open to visitors. Eisenhower State Recreation Area is on the south shore near the dam.

The Texas Legislature decided in 1947 that there should be a state park on this new lake and that it should be named for Dwight Eisenhower. It was before Eisenhower was elected president. He was still in the Army, but there was plenty of reason to name a park for him. He was a hero of the first order and he had been born in Denison just a few miles from the park. Eisenhower was president by the time the state actually bought the 457 acres for this park in 1954.

This is limestone country. The timber runs more to scrub than to forest. There are several species of oak, ash and American and cedar elm. Part of the park is grassy prairie.

Most of the park sits high above the lake and the shore line is more cliff than beach, but the park offers a boat ramp, a swimming beach, a fish-cleaning shelter and four fishing piers. This is one of the biggest lakes in the state and there are many big boats here at the Eisenhower Yacht Club. The club is operated by a concessionaire. He sells camping supplies and foods, but his main business is berthing and servicing boats owned mostly by people from Dallas and Fort Worth. The boathouses take up a substantial part of the water frontage in the park.

Sailing and skiing are popular sports here. The lake is most famous for the native Red River white bass, but there are black bass, striped bass, crappie and catfish in Lake Texoma, too. Visitors may see white-tail deer, raccoons and grey foxes in the woods and many species of wild birds.

Eisenhower Park has 35 screened shelters for rent with water, electricity, table and grill. They are on a bluff above the lake and near a fishing pier. The fee is $8 a night. There are 48 campsites with water, table, grill and tent pad at $4 a

Some of the campsites in the Eisenhower State Recreation Area on the south of Lake Texoma lack shade, but the screened shelters here are well shaded and some of them are right over the lake.

night; 45 campsites with water, electricity, table, grill and tent pad at $6 a night; and 50 trailer campsites with water, electricity, sewer hookup, table and grill at $7 a night.

The large recreation hall here has central heat and air, 10 tables, 100 chairs, range, refrigerator, oven and indoor restrooms. The rent is $55 for day use only, up to 100 people. The fee for overnight use, for up to 48 people, is $85. There is also a group campground with an open-air pavillion, picnic tables and 37 campsites for $6 each per night.

For more information

You can make reservations or get more information about Eisenhower State Recreation Area by writing the Superintendent, Rt. 2, Box 50K, Denison, TX 75020. The phone number is (214) 465-1956.

Other places to see

Also in this area are the house where President Eisenhower was born at 208 East Day Street in Denison, the Bonham State Recreation Area south of Bonham, the home of the late Congressman Sam Rayburn on U.S. 82 just west of Bonham and the Sam Rayburn Library in downtown Bonham.

EISENHOWER BIRTHPLACE STATE HISTORIC SITE

208 East Day Street, just east of U.S. 75 in Denison in Grayson County, 77 miles north of Dallas.
Fees: adults $1, children 25¢

Denison was an important railroad town in the late 1800s. David Eisenhower brought his family here in 1888 when he went to work for the Missouri, Kansas and Texas Railroad. The family moved into this house near the tracks. Dwight David Eisenhower was born here October 14, 1890, but the family moved again before Dwight was a year old. Denison did not make much impression on him.

A Denison school principal named Jennie Jackson thought the name Dwight David Eisenhower sounded familiar when she began hearing it during World War II. She remembered helping take care of a boy by that name when she was a young girl in Denison. Jennie Jackson wrote to Gen. Eisenhower and asked him if he was born in Denison. The general wrote back that she should write his mother because he was not sure where he was born. Jennie Jackson wrote to Mrs. Eisenhower and she confirmed that the general was born in this house on East Day Street in Denison.

The family was always more attached to Kansas. The other five Eisenhower boys were born there. The president always regarded Abilene as his home town, but Jennie Jackson claimed Ike for Denison. She helped organize a group to buy and preserve the house on East Day. The group deeded the property to the city of Denison. The city deeded it in 1953 to the Eisenhower Birthplace Foundation. The foundation moved several other houses away and put in landscaping and a parking lot and then deeded the property to the State Parks Board in 1958.

The house has been restored and furnished the way such a house probably would have been furnished in 1890. The only item in the house that actually belonged to the Eisenhower family is a quilt in the room where the president was born. An antique phone in the hall plays a message Gen. Eisenhower recorded in 1952.

The Eisenhower Birthplace is open for conducted tours every day except Christmas and New Year's. The hours are 8 a.m. to 5 p.m. in the summer and 10 a.m. to 5 p.m. the rest of the year.

For more information

Arrangements for group tours should be made with the Superintendent, 208 East Day Street, Denison, TX 75020. The phone number is (214) 465-8908.

Other places to see

The Eisenhower State Recreation Area is 7 miles northwest of Denison off F.M. 1310. The Sam Rayburn Library and the late Congressman Sam Rayburn's home are in Bonham, 28 miles southeast on U.S. 82.

The late President Eisenhower was a five-star general before he learned that he was born in Denison, in this house at 208 East Day Street. The house is open for tours every day except Christmas and New Year's Day.

BONHAM STATE RECREATION AREA

3 miles south of Bonham off State Highway 78 on F.M. 271 in Fannin County, 73 miles northeast of Dallas.
Entrance fee: $2 per car

The city of Bonham donated 261 acres of land to the State Parks Board in 1934. The National Park Service drew up the plans and the CCC built this park. You don't have to know a lot about politics to know what influenced the decisions on where the parks were built during the early years of the Roosevelt New Deal. You can understand why one was built here when you realize who was representing this district in Congress at the time. The congressman was Sam Rayburn. He was not yet Speaker of the House. He was not even elected majority leader until 1937, but Rayburn had been in Congress 20 years when the CCC program began and he was one of the members to be reckoned with in the House of Representatives.

The Bonham State Recreation Area has the features usually found in the CCC parks — a small lake with a sturdy shelter and bathhouse and a small swimming beach. The lake is only 65 acres; so only small boats are allowed and the speed limit is 5 miles per hour. There is a boat ramp and dock. A concessionaire rents canoes and pedal boats.

This park is less heavily wooded than some of the other East Texas parks. Part of the park is grassy prairie with substantial displays of wildflowers in the spring. The trees are oak, cedar, cottonwood, black willow and green ash. The foliage is colorful in the fall.

This park has a group mess hall, with barracks accommodating up to 96 people, for rent at $100 a night. A group picnic shelter rents for $8 a day for parties up to 25. Parties of 26 or more pay $16. This shelter is not available overnight.

A small lake is the chief attraction in the Bonham State Recreation Area. The Civilian Conservation Corps created the lake and built the original buildings here in the 1930s. This is a small park and visitors seldom see animals any bigger than raccoons here.

There are 10 campsites with water, table and grill for $4 a night and 11 campsites with water, electricity, table and grill for $6 a night. The campsites are all near the lake. There are 14 picnic sites near the lake and 15 sites in the woods.

For more information

You can make reservations or get more information about Bonham State Recreation Area from the Superintendent, Rt. 1, Box 337, Bonham, TX 75418 or phone (214) 583-5022.

Other places to see

Some other places you may want to see in this area are the Sam Rayburn Library on U.S. 82 in downtown Bonham; the home of the late Speaker Rayburn, maintained as a museum by the Texas Historical Commission, about a mile west of Bonham on U.S. 82; the Flying Tiger Museum, a collection of World War II airplanes, on U.S. 82 about 35 miles east of Bonham; and the Sam Bell Maxey State Historic Structure at 812 South Church Street in Paris, 37 miles east of Bonham.

SAM BELL MAXEY HOUSE STATE HISTORIC STRUCTURE

812 South Church Street in Paris in Lamar County, 110 miles northeast of Dallas. Fees: adults $1, children 25¢

This home was built in 1867 by a prosperous lawyer and politician and has been preserved with the additions and modifications made over almost a hundred years by his heirs.

The home was built for Sam Bell Maxey. He and his father moved their families here from Kentucky in 1857. Both men were lawyers. Sam was soon elected district attorney. He had been educated at West Point, where he was a classmate of Ulysses Grant, and he had served with the U.S. Army in the Mexican War. Lamar County voted against secession, but Sam volunteered for the Confederate Army when the war began. He was a major general when the war ended. He resumed his law practice and started building this house two years later.

Mrs. Maxey managed the household here between 1874 and 1887 while Sam served two terms in the U.S. Senate. The Maxeys had no children; so the house passed to the son of one of Sam's nieces after Sam and Mrs. Maxey died. Sam Bell Maxey Long and his wife did some major remodeling in 1911. Long died in 1948 and his wife in 1965. Her cousin, Alice Fairfax Stone, inherited the house then.

Alice Fairfax Stone gave the house to the Lamar County Historical Society in 1967. The society maintained the house as a museum until 1972 and then gave it to the city of Paris. The city deeded the property to the Parks and Wildlife Department in 1976. The department opened the house to the public in 1980.

The Sam Bell Maxey house is what is known as High Victorian Italianate style. It stood originally on a five-acre site with gardens and stables and several other outbuildings. The site has been reduced now to two acres. The house and grounds are maintained with the care that has characterized the Parks and Wildlife operations in recent years. The Paris Council of Garden Clubs decorates the house in

The Sam Bell Maxey house has been standing here at the corner of Church and Washington streets in Paris since 1868. It has been part of the state park system since 1980.

Victorian style at Christmas time, so this probably is the best season to visit.

The Sam Bell Maxey house is open for guided tours from 10 a.m. to 5 p.m. every day except Monday and Tuesday. The furnishings are pieces the Maxeys and their heirs used. Many of the family photographs, letters, toys and keepsakes are still in the house.

For more information

You can get more information about the Sam Bell Maxey house by phoning (214) 785-5716 or by writing to the Superintendent, Sam Bell Maxey House, 812 South Church Street, Paris, TX 75460.

Other places to see

Some other places you may want to see in this area are Bonham State Recreation Area about 40 miles east on F.M. 271 south of Bonham; the home of the late House Speaker Sam Rayburn on U.S. 82 about 1 mile west of Bonham; the Sam Rayburn Library in downtown Bonham; the Flying Tiger Museum, a collection of World War II airplanes, on U.S. 82 about 2 miles west of Paris and the Gambill Goose Refuge on Lake Gibbons, F.M. 79 at F.M. 2820, about 10 miles northwest of Paris. Oklahoma is just 18 miles north of Paris.

GOVERNOR HOGG SHRINE STATE HISTORICAL PARK

On State Highway 37, just south of downtown Quitman in Wood County, 91 miles east of Dallas.
Fees: adults $1, children 25¢

This park is a tribute to the first native Texan to be governor of Texas. James Stephen Hogg was born outside Rusk in Cherokee County in 1851. He was married to Sarah Ann Stinson here in Quitman in 1874. Hogg was elected governor in 1890 and served two terms. He did some speculating in real estate and oil properties after he left the governor's office. A major oil field discovered after he died in 1906 on a plantation he had bought in 1901 made his children very rich. Gov. and Mrs. Hogg had three sons and one daughter before Mrs. Hogg died in 1895. The daughter was named Ima for the main character in a poem the governor's brother had written. Ima never had a sister, regardless of what you may have heard.

Ima Hogg was devoted to her father, probably in part because her mother had died when she was only three. She inherited her father's humanity and concern for the public welfare. She passed most of the material things she bought with her fortune on to the people of Texas. This park is just one example. The site is the old Wood County Reunion Grounds. Old settlers and their descendants still meet here every August, but the property was deeded to the state in 1946. Two houses and a small museum are located on the grounds.

The larger house was built in 1869 on another site nearby. It was the home of Sarah Ann Stinson's parents. Sarah Ann and James Hogg were married in this house. It later was the home of a family named Andrews, and Sallie Lucie Andrews Old donated it to the state.

Ima Hogg had the Stinson house moved to the park in 1969 and she donated or paid for most of the furnishings. The smaller house here is a replica of the house James and Sarah Hogg lived in right after they were married. Ima Hogg helped pay for the house and the furnishings. Some of the furnishings are old Hogg family possessions.

The Ima Hogg Museum was added to the park in 1969. The exhibits in the museum depict some of the history of Wood County. The houses and the museum are open for tours every day except Tuesdays and Wednesdays from 9 a.m. till noon and 1 p.m. till 4 p.m. There is no fee for admission to the park. The fees for the tours are $1 for adults and 25 cents for children.

You may think there is nothing very remarkable about either of the two houses here, but appreciation of the Hogg family is likely to grow through the years. Gov.

One of the houses in the Governor Hogg Shrine State Historical Park is a replica of the cottage where Jim and Sarah Ann Hogg spent their honeymoon in 1874. The house where they were married is also in the park. The houses are open for tours every day except Tuesdays and Wednesdays.

Hogg curbed land speculators, pushed through the act creating the Texas Railroad Commission to rein in the railroad promoters and came down harder on special interests than is usual in Texas.

There is a story that Gov. Hogg once said the only monuments he wanted were trees on his grave, but three state parks commemorate his life and career — this one; the Jim Hogg State Historical Park at Rusk, where he was born; and the Varner-Hogg Plantation at West Columbia where he lived the last years of his life. Ima Hogg had something to do with all three.

For more information

You can get more information about the Governor Hogg Shrine Historical Park and the tours from the Superintendent, Rt. 3, Quitman, TX 75783. The telephone number is (214) 763-2701.

Other places to see

Tyler State Park is 45 miles southeast on F.M. 16 just west of F.M. 14. The Municipal Rose Garden and the Goodman-LeGrand House Museum on North Broadway in Tyler are also interesting.

DAINGERFIELD STATE PARK

On State Highway 49, 2 miles east of Daingerfield in Morris County, 142 miles northeast of Dallas.
Entrance fee: $2 per car

Texans living west of I-45 sometimes wonder what anyone sees in East Texas. This is a good place to start finding out. Many of the physical features that give East Texas its special charm and character are captured and preserved in this park and the parks at Atlanta, Caddo Lake and Tyler.

Daingerfield State Park has a small lake surrounded by 550 acres of pine and hardwood. The CCC built the lake, the bathhouse and the original group shelter here in 1935. The park opened to the public in 1938. A number of improvements have been made since then and the park is a very pleasant family resort.

The lake is only 80 acres; so no large boats are allowed and the boat speed limit is 5 miles per hour. There is a boat ramp and dock and a concessionaire has small boats for rent. The park store has some camping supplies for sale. The store is open only during the summer.

The park has a swimming beach, two fishing piers, fish-cleaning tables, a playground and an amphitheater. There is a hiking trail around the lake. Hikers may see a variety of birds including the red-cockaded woodpecker and the pileated woodpecker. Squirrels, foxes and a few deer live in the woods. The best times to visit here probably are the fall when the hardwoods turn red and the spring when the dogwood trees are in bloom.

Daingerfield has 23 picnic sites. The Mountain View Campground here has 15 campsites with water, table and grill for $4 a night. The Dogwood Campground has 16 sites with water, electricity, table and grill for $6 a night. The Big Pine Campground has nine trailer campsites with water, electricity, sewer connections, table and grill for $7 a night. The park also has three cabins and a group lodge. Two of the cabins sleep four people each; the third can sleep six. The Bass Lodge holds up to 20 and rents for $65 a night. Rates for the smaller cabins are $18

The little lake in Daingerfield State Park is open only to canoes, pedal boats and very small motorboats. There are several stone and log cabins in this park built by the CCC in the 1930s.

a night for one or two people, plus another $4 for each additional adult and $1 for each child between 6 and 12. Children under 6 stay free.

Daingerfield Park was named for the town of Daingerfield, which was named for early settler London Daingerfield. There is a lot of iron ore in this part of East Texas. Iron foundries here made equipment and ammunition for the Confederacy during the Civil War. A blast furnace from those days still stands on the grounds of the Lone Star Steel Company at Lone Star, 7 miles south of Daingerfield.

For more information

You can make reservations or get more information about this park by writing the Superintendent, Rt. 1, Box 286-B, Daingerfield, TX 75638 or by phoning (214) 645-2921.

Other places to see

The people of Cass County, just east of this park, are proud of their wildflowers. You should make the drive on State Highway 11 east to Linden, then southwest on State Highway 155 to Avinger, then north to Hughes Springs if you happen to be here in April.

Some other places you may want to see in this area are Atlanta State Recreation Area about 50 miles northeast off F.M. 1154; the old river port city of Jefferson, 32 miles to the southeast on State Highway 49 (Excelsior House and many historic buildings); and Caddo Lake State Park, 13 miles farther to the southeast on F.M. 2198.

ATLANTA STATE RECREATION AREA

12 miles northwest of Atlanta off F.M. 1154 in Cass County, 183 miles northeast of Dallas. Entrance fee: $2 per car

The Atlanta State Recreation Area is on the south shore of a lake the Army Corps of Engineers built in 1957 to conserve water and control flooding. The lake was created by damming the Sulphur River. It was called Texarkana Reservoir when it was completed, but the name was changed to Lake Wright Patman after Congressman Wright Patman died in 1976. Patman had represented this district in the U.S. House of Representatives for 48 years. The lake covers almost 120,000 acres; so the opportunities for water sports are unlimited here.

The park opened in 1958 on 1,475 acres leased from the Corps of Engineers. There are bass, crappie and catfish in the lake. The park has two boat ramps, a swimming beach, a playground, a hiking trail, a nature trail and a mini-bike trail. A few other state parks have mini-bike trails, too, but no state park has any trails for other types of motorbikes. Motorbikes that are legal on the streets are allowed on the parks roads, but not the trails. The fee is the same as for cars, $2.

Most of the park here is covered by oak and pine forest. Dogwood makes a show in the spring. There are 40 picnic sites. The group picnic site rents for $8 a day for up to 25 people; $16 for more than 25. It is for day use only. The park has eight campsites with water for $4 a day; 43 sites with water and electricity for $6 a day; and eight sites with water, electricity and sewer connections for $7 a day. There are no screened shelters or cabins in this park.

For more information

The address for reservations or more information is Superintendent, Altanta State Recreation Area, Rt. 1, Box 116, Atlanta, TX 75551. The telephone number is (214) 796-6476.

Other places to see

Other interesting places in this area are Daingerfield State Park, 50 miles southwest on State Highway 11; the old river port of Jefferson, 37 miles south on State Highway 49; Caddo Lake State Park about 50 miles south on F.M. 2198; and the city of Texarkana about 34 miles north on U.S. 59 (Texarkana Historical Museum, 219 State Line Avenue; Perot Theater, Main Street at Third).

There are some very pretty picnic sites overlooking Lake Wright Patman in the Atlanta State Recreation Area.

CADDO LAKE STATE PARK

15 miles northeast of Marshall off State Highway 43 on F.M. 2198 in Harrison County, 169 miles east of Dallas. Entrance fee: $2 per car

I could live happily the year-round in the Caddo Lake State Park. The cabins are some of the most comfortable the parks system has. The lake is full of fish. The scenery is as picturesque as any in the state; the atmosphere is tranquilizing. But the Parks and Wildlife Department has rules to prevent people like me from becoming permanent lodgers. One of the rules is that visitors cannot stay more than two weeks at a time.

Caddo Lake was here before the white man came. The Caddo Indians thought this lake was created by an earthquake because one of their chiefs failed to obey the wishes of the Great Spirit. An earthquake may have had something to do with it. A great logjam on the Red River also had something to do with it. The lake is one of the biggest natural lakes in the South. It was bigger before the Army Engineers dynamited that logjam on the Red River in the late 1800s. The engineers later built a dam at Mooringsport, Louisiana, to impound the present lake, but the water level is lower than it was and the once-busy river port of Jefferson is a river port no more.

The streams feeding Caddo Lake are Big Cypress Bayou and Little Cypress Bayou. The park fronts on Big Cypress Bayou. A boat ramp gives access to miles of mysterious water trails and fishing holes. The water in the bayou at the park is also suitable for skiing. Park concessionaires David and Kathy Lomax have canoes and camping equipment for rent and they also provide a guide service for people unfamiliar with the labyrinth of waterways here.

The park was established in 1934. The CCC built the roads, the recreation hall and the cabins. The nine cabins were rebuilt in the late 1960s. They all have kitchenettes with electric ranges, bathrooms with showers, air conditioning and heat. Two of the cabins have just one double bed each, with a limit of two people per cabin. Four have two double beds each with a limit of four people. Three have two double beds each, plus a sofa that makes into a double bed. The limit on these is six people per cabin. Towels, sheets and blankets are furnished; dishes and cooking utensils are not. These cabins rent for $18 a night for one or two people. Additional adults pay $4 each; additional children (6-12) are $1 each. There is no charge for children under 6.

The park also has eight screened shelters for rent at $8 a night with water, electricity, a table and grill. There are 20 campsites with water for $4 a night; 20 campsites with water and electricity for $6 a night; and eight trailer campsites with water, electricity for sewer connections for $7 a night. All these campsites have tables and grills. The restrooms in the camping areas have showers.

A large recreation hall near the cabins is available for reunions and meetings at $40 a day, or it can be rented overnight for $70. There are no provisions for cooking and no bedding. The hall will accommodate 100 people in the daytime, 48 overnight.

The park has a playground, a fishing pier, picnic sites and a nature trail. The visitor center has displays illustrating some of the history and natural history of the area. The visitor center also has leaflets to help hikers identify the trees they will see on the nature trail. Observant hikers may also see some white-tailed deer, possums, raccoons and alligators.

For more information

You can make reservations or get more information about this park by writing the Superintendent, Rt. 2, Box 15, Karnack, TX 75661. The phone number is (214) 679-3351. The phone number for reserving canoes or arranging for guides is (214) 935-2723.

Other places to see

Other places of interest in this area are Karnack about 3 miles south on State Highway 43 (the house where Lady Bird Johnson lived as a girl); Marshall, 17 miles southwest on State Highway 43 (Ginnochio Hotel and several historic homes); and Jefferson, 14 miles northeast on F.M. 134 (Jefferson Historical Museum, Excelsior House, many historic homes and buildings).

There are several good and informal catfish restaurants around Caddo Lake.

MARTIN CREEK LAKE STATE RECREATION AREA

Off State Highway 43 west of Tatum about 23 miles southeast of Longview in Rusk County, 153 miles southeast of Dallas. No fee

Martin Creek Park is a state park only in name. Texas Utilities built a power plant a few years ago to use the local lignite for fuel. The power company built a small lake to provide cooling water for the generating plant and built a small park on the lake. The power company deeded the 216 acres here to the state in 1976.

The park has a small swimming beach and two boat ramps. There is a picnic area and a sign saying that camping is not allowed. People camp here anyway because there is no one to stop them. The Parks and Wildlife Department is planning some improvements, but the department had no staff on the grounds in the summer of 1984.

The water in the Martin Creek Reservoir is quite warm. Local fishermen say bass thrive in it. *Texas Fisherman* editor Larry Bozka says this about Martin Creek Reservoir: "This lake is a good bet for trophy bassing in the springtime. Worm fishing is the rule (grape or red plastic worms during the colder months, switching to chartreuse spinnerbaits or crankbaits during the spring spawn). Post-spawn fish will hit spinnerbaits and topwaters."

There is little besides fishing to attract visitors to this park at this time.

Opposite Top: The comfortable log cabins in Caddo Lake State Park have heat and air conditioning and they are available the year round. This park covers 480 acres on Big Cypress Bayou.

Opposite Bottom: There is a picture everywhere you look in this park. *Texas Fisherman* editor Larry Bozka says the best time for fishing here is early morning and the best places are around the cypress trees in shallow water. Crappie fishing with minnows and bobbers is the most productive.

Top: This park is being administered by the Parks and Wildlife Department Region III Office, Rt. 9, Tyler, TX 75706.

TYLER STATE PARK

On F.M. 14, 8 miles north of Tyler, 2 miles north of I-20 in Smith County, 91 miles southeast of Dallas.
Entrance fee: $2 per car

The property for Tyler State Park was acquired from 16 individual property owners by Smith County and the city of Tyler. The National Park Service drew the plans and the CCC built the park.

The park covers 985 acres of pine and hardwood forest and includes a small lake stocked with black bass and channel catfish. There are two fishing piers, docks, a boat ramp and boathouse. Small boats can be rented at the boathouse during the summer. No large boats are allowed here. There is a bathhouse and swimming beach, but no lifeguards. The concession building on the lakefront has a stone terrace plenty big enough for dances.

The Tyler park is a beauty spot any time of year. It is at its best in the spring when the dogwood is in bloom and in the fall when the hardwoods are changing color. There is a nature trail and a variety of wildlife and birds. Deer, raccoons, possums, Bobwhites, doves and many woodland birds live here year round and many other bird species migrate through here.

The park has an amphitheater, a mini-bike trail and an unusually large number of campsites. There are four tent camping areas with a total of 41 campsites at $4 a night. Two other camping areas have a total of 38 sites with water and electricity for $6 a night. A trailer camping area has 38 sites with water, electricity and sewer connections at $7 a night. A group trailer camping area has 29 sites.

The park has no cabins, but there is a cluster of 29 screened shelters near the lake. Each shelter has water, electricity, table and grill and rents for $8 a night. A group picnic shelter with kitchen rents for $60 a day. The restrooms in the camping areas have showers.

The 48 individual picnic tables here are all available on a first come, first served basis, as they are in all the state parks. There is no fee for individual picnic sites.

The park and the campgrounds are open year round. They are not very crowded in the winter months, but some of our winter Texans often stop for a few days in these East Texas parks on their travels between the Middle West and the Valley.

For more information

You can make reservations or get more information about Tyler State Park by writing to the Superintendent, Rt. 9, Tyler, TX 75706 or by calling (214) 597-5338.

Other places to see

In the city of Tyler, you may want to visit the Municipal Rose Garden on State Highway 31 at Fair Park Drive or the Goodman-LeGrand house at 624 North Broadway, 8 miles south of the park on F.M. 14.

The little lake in Tyler State Park is fed by springs. It is stocked with channel catfish and black bass. Only small boats are allowed.

JIM HOGG STATE HISTORICAL PARK

1 mile east of Rusk on State Highway 84 in Cherokee County, 130 miles southeast of Dallas. No entrance fee

James Stephen Hogg was the first native Texan to be elected governor of Texas and this is where he was born.

Joseph and Lucanda Hogg moved to Texas from Alabama in 1839. They settled first in Nacogdoches and moved here a few years later. They had two daughters when they came to Texas. Three sons were born in Texas. The Hoggs had a plantation they called Mountain Home here outside Rusk when James Hogg was born in 1851. The young Hoggs lost both their parents during the Civil War. Joseph Hogg died of natural causes while serving as a brigadier general with Confederate forces in Mississippi in 1862. Lucanda Hogg died here at the plantation in 1863. The younger Hoggs sold off the family estate as they struggled to make a living and get an education after the war. The city of Rusk acquired this much of the plantation years later and deeded it to the state in 1941 to be maintained as a park. The original Hogg home had burned in 1937. The deed transferring the property to the state stipulated that a replica of the Hogg home was to be built on the site.

The house here now is not represented as being an exact replica. It is described as a house typical of this area at the time the Hoggs were living here. It is furnished and maintained as a museum. The park is open every day. The museum is open from 10 a.m. to noon and 1 p.m. to 4 p.m. from March 1 through November 30. The museum probably is on the site of the original Hogg house. A family cemetery is nearby, but neither Gov. Hogg nor his father is buried in this cemetery. Gov. Hogg is buried in Austin. His father is buried in Mississippi.

There are no provisions for camping in this park, but there are some picnic sites and there is a hiking trail. The park covers only 177 acres, but it is pretty and very well kept. This is a nice side trip for anyone camping at the Rusk-Palestine State Park or at Mission Tejas.

For more information

You can get more information about the Jim Hogg State Historical Park or arrange special tours by writing the Superintendent, Rt. 2, Box 29, Rusk, TX 75785. The phone number is (214) 683-4850.

Other places to see

Some other places you may want to visit in this area are the Rusk-Palestine State Park and Texas State Railroad on U.S. 84, 3 miles west of Rusk; Caddoan Mounds State Historic Site off State Highway 21, 18 miles south of Rusk; Mission Tejas State Historical Park off State Highway 21, 24 miles south of Rusk; Nacogdoches (Millard's Crossing and many historic buildings), 36 miles southeast of Rusk on State Highway 21. No highway in Texas has more historical markers than State Highway 21. This is the old Camino Real, also called the Old San Antonio Road, from colonial days.

The museum on the grounds of the Jim Hogg State Historical Park has a number of pioneer artifacts and a bed and dresser that belonged to the Hogg family.

RUSK-PALESTINE STATE PARK AND TEXAS STATE RAILROAD HISTORICAL PARK

Rusk unit, 3 miles west of Rusk on U.S. 84 in Cherokee County; Palestine unit, 6 miles east of Palestine on U.S. 84 in Anderson County, 130 miles southeast of Dallas. No entrance fee

The state of Texas built this railroad in 1896 to haul ore from the Palestine area to a foundry the prison system was then operating at Rusk. The right of way is substantially the same now as then. Everything else has changed. The prison foundry closed in 1913. The tracks were rented out and the state went out of the railroad business until 1972.

The Parks and Wildlife Department took over the tracks in 1972 and started buying up some antique rolling stock. Depots were built on the east side of Palestine and on the west side of Rusk, 25 miles apart. The city of Palestine established a park around the depot on the Palestine end; the city of Rusk established a park on the Rusk end of the line. The Texas State Railroad was an instant success. The Parks and Wildlife Department took over operation of the parks at each end of the line in 1982. These two parks make up the Rusk-Palestine State Park. The Texas State Railroad Historical Park is a separate entity on paper, but it ties the two units of Rusk-Palestine together.

The locomotives the Texas State Railroad uses are authentic old steam engines. There are five of them. Two were built in 1917. The others were built in 1896, 1901 and 1911. The trains run Wednesday through Sunday during the summer (May to August). They run only on weekends in the spring (March to May) and in the fall (September to mid-November). There are only two trains a day. One leaves the depot at Palestine at 11 a.m. on operating days and the other one leaves the depot at Rusk at the same time. The train from Palestine reaches the Rusk depot at 12:30. The train from Rusk reaches the Palestine depot at the same time. There is a layover of one hour. The Palestine train leaves Rusk on the return trip to Palestine at 1:30 and arrives at 3 p.m. The Rusk train leaves Palestine on the

Left: The Parks and Wildlife Department requires a deposit on train tickets reserved more than 10 days in advance. There is no deposit on tickets reserved less than 10 days, but these tickets will be put on sale if they are not picked up at least an hour before departure. There are no reserved seats.

Opposite: The train from Palestine approaching Maydelle on the run to Rusk.

return trip to Rusk at the same time and arrives at 3 p.m. This schedule gives passengers several options. They can buy round-trip tickets at either end and go the whole distance or they can buy a one-way ticket at either end and have someone pick them up in a car at the other end. U.S. 84 roughly parallels the tracks. A car can cover the distance between the two depots in about a third the time the train takes. Train tickets are $4 one way and $6 round trip for adults, $2.50 one way and $4 round trip for children (3-12).

There are pleasant picnic grounds in both parks and snack shops in both depots. Many visitors carry their own picnic lunches on the train. More elaborate parties are possible. You can charter one of the trains for $1,500. The department also rents them to movie crews sometimes.

The trains travel though woods most of the distance. The tracks cross several small streams and the Neches River. Riders occasionally get to see a deer, raccoon, possum or armadillo. Old railroad men appreciate steam trains more than most people. You may meet one of them on just about any trip you make on the Texas State Railroad. Ask the conductor if one is aboard, if you would like to hear some stories about the old days. Old railroad men usually like to talk, and the conductors usually know if there is one aboard.

Three hours on a train may be a bit much for small children and people traveling with youngsters may want to ride just one way. But I have heard very few complaints about the length of the trip or any other aspect of this operation. I think the best way to get the most enjoyment out of the experience is to get at least two carloads of people together and drive to either depot and split up into two groups. One group can ride the train to the other end of the line. The other group can drive a car and take lunch and have it all set up and waiting when the train arrives. The two groups can then change places for the trip back. Everybody will have the experience and no one will have an overdose.

There are several vantage points along U.S. 84 where you can get a good look at the trains or take a picture. The little town of Maydelle is a good vantage point. There is a station, but the trains don't stop at Maydelle.

The Palestine unit of the Rusk-Palestine State Park has no provisions for cam-

ping. There is a large parking lot, restrooms and picnic shelters.

The Rusk unit is larger. It covers 100 acres. The small lake is stocked with bass, perch and catfish. There are several picnic sites, a pavillion, a fishing pier on the lake, a playground and two free tennis courts. A wooded campground in the Rusk unit has 16 tent sites with water, electricity, table and grill for $6 a night; 46 group trailer sites with water, electricity, table and grill for $6 a night; and 32 trailer sites with water, electricity, table, grill and sewer connections for $7 a night. A group shelter is available for day use only at $50 a day.

For more information

You need reservations for the train trip. The toll free number is 1-800-442-8951, or you can write Texas State Railroad, Box 39, Rusk, TX 75785. The number for reserving campsites is (214) 683-5126. You can also make reservations or get more information about the Rusk-Palestine State Park by writing the Superintendent, Rt. 4, Box 431, Rusk, TX 75785.

Other places to see

Other interesting places in this area are Palestine (several historic homes, Dogwood Trail in the spring); Rusk (Jim Hogg State Historical Park, 1 mile east of U.S. 69 on U.S. 84); Nacogdoches (Old Stone Fort on campus of Stephen F. Austin State University and several historic buildings), 36 miles southeast of Rusk on State Highway 21; Caddoan Mounds State Historic Site, 18 miles south of Rusk on State Highway 21; and Mission Tejas State Historical Park, 8 miles west of Caddoan Mounds on State Highway 21.

CADDOAN MOUNDS STATE HISTORIC SITE

On State Highway 21, 6 miles west of Alto in Cherokee County, 148 miles southeast of Dallas. No entrance fee. Tour fees: adults $1, children 25¢

The early inhabitants of Texas were nowhere near as advanced as the Incas, Mayas or Aztecs. The Caddos were about the most sophisticated people to live in this part of the world before the Europeans came. The Caddos were farmers and traders. They occupied an area centered in what is now Arkansas. This site was on the outer edge of their territory.

There is some evidence that other tribes may have occupied this site as early as 10,000 B.C. The Caddos were here from 780 A.D. to about 1260 A.D. A later Caddo culture may have lived here for a while, but most of the artifacts found here are attributed to the 780-1260 A.D. period.

The presence of these mounds was mentioned by Athanase de Mezieres in his report on an expedition he made in 1779 for the King of Spain. He recognized the mounds as remnants of an early Indian settlement. The first professional archaelogical investigation was made in 1919 by J.E. Pearce for the Bureau of Ethnology.

The first systematic excavation was done in 1939-1941 by H.P. Newell of the University of Texas, working with a grant from the WPA. He excavated about half of what has been identified as the High Temple Mound. U.T. crews directed by Dee Anne Story began excavating the Low Temple Mound and the Burial Mound in 1968. The Parks and Wildlife Department bought 70 acres of the old Indian city in 1974 and another 23 acres in 1981. The exploration has been continuing and it is apparent that the settlement was bigger than first thought. Archaeologists and students from the University of Texas are often here working and visitors are encouraged to watch and ask questions.

The Caddos apparently were the first Texas farmers. Researchers think they know what kind of houses they built and how they built them. The Parks and Wildlife Department has built such a house on the site; it is part of the park tour.

The depot at the Palestine end of the Texas State Railroad is surrounded by a small park with picnic tables, but no campground.

There is no fee for access to the park, but the tours are $1 for adults and 25 cents for children. The tours begin with an exhibit of artifacts and murals illustrating what life among the Caddoans may have been like. There is an audiovisual presentation. The tour around the grounds is self-guided.

The park is open only five days a week from 8 a.m. to 5 p.m. It is closed Mondays and Tuesdays. There are no provisions for camping or picnicking here and the law forbids any amateur excavating in this or any other Texas state park.

For more information

You can make arrangements for group tours or get more information about Caddoan Mounds from the Superintendent, Rt. 2, Box 85C, Alto, TX 75925. The phone number is (409) 858-3218.

Other places to see

Several places you may want to see in this area are Mission Tejas State Historical Park, 8 miles southwest on State Highway 21; Crockett, 28 miles southwest on State Highway 21 (the Monroe Crook House, 707 East Houston); Jim Hogg State Historical Park, 19 miles north on U.S. 84, 1 mile east of U.S. 69; and Rusk-Palestine State Park, 21 miles north on U.S. 84, 3 miles west of U.S. 69.

Left: Parks and Wildlife Department experts put a lot of time and effort into creating what they believe is an authentic replica of a Caddoan house. Visitors aren't allowed in it anymore since it was damaged by Hurricane Alicia in 1983.

Opposite: The mission replica in the Mission Tejas State Historical Park is what an early Spanish mission might have looked like if it had been built by Anglos.

MISSION TEJAS STATE HISTORICAL PARK

21 miles northeast of Crockett on State Highway 21 in Houston County, 160 miles southeast of Dallas. Entrance fee: $2 per car

This park is in the Davy Crockett National Forest and it is believed to be on the site of the first mission the Spanish built in Texas. The Spanish built missions as much to advertise their claim to the territory as to minister to the Indians. Anxiety about the French presence in Louisiana led the Spanish Franciscans to establish the Mission San Francisco de los Tejas in 1690. The Indians did not take very kindly to the idea. The missionaries gave up in 1693. They burned their mission and went back to Mexico. The mission was reestablished in 1716 at another site a little farther east. It was abandoned in 1719, established again in 1721 and then abandoned again a few years later. The Franciscans put their energies after that into establishing in San Antonio the mission we still know as San Francisco de la Espada.

No one is sure exactly where the second Mission Tejas was, but the discovery of an old Spanish cannon where this park is caused early settlers to believe the original 1690 mission was here. Some Houston County residents organized a move to get the area designated a park in the 1930s when the federal government was helping states develop parks through the CCC. The CCC built the little log church that commemorates the original mission. It is not represented as an exact replica. The logs are laid horizontally and the building has a number of windows. The idea of laying logs horizontally came to Texas with the Anglos. A log building built here in 1690 surely would have the logs laid vertically and there would have been minimum openings, but it looks the way people expect log buildings to look. The Texas Forest Service maintained the mission park until 1957 when the Parks and Wildlife Department took it over.

An authentic old log building was moved into the park in 1974. The Joseph Rice house was built outside Crockett on what is now State Highway 21 in 1828. It was a single room until Rice started adding onto it in the 1830s. He added two more rooms, a dog trot and porches. He raised a large family in the house and also boarded travelers. Rice's descendants lived in the house until 1919. It was used as a barn and garage then until 1973 when Mrs. John Rice donated it to the state. The Parks and Wildlife Department restored it and it stands near the entrance to this park now as an example of what housing was like in early Texas.

Mission Tejas Park is 118 acres of pine forest with a very small lake. Fishing in the lake is restricted to children 12 years of age and younger. There is a playground, a nature trail and a hiking trail. A group picnic shelter is available at $8 a day for groups up to 25; groups of 26 or more pay $16. The shelter can accommodate up to 150 people. There are two camping areas. One has three sites with water for $4 a day. The other has seven sites with water and electricity for $6 a day, and five sites with full hookups for $7. This park is very pretty in late March and early April when the dogwoods are in bloom.

For more information

You can make reservations or get more information about Mission Tejas Park by writing the Superintendent, Rt. 2, Box 108, Grapeland, TX 75844. The phone number is (409) 687-2394.

Other places to see

Other sites you may be interested in seeing in this area are Crockett, 21 miles southwest of State Highway 21 (Monroe Crook house, 707 East Houston, and other historic homes); Caddoan Mounds State Historic Site, 8 miles northeast on State Highway 21; and Nacogdoches, 37 miles northeast on State Highway 21 (Sterne house at 211 South Lanana and many other historic buildings).

The parents of these youngsters say Fairfield Lake State Recreation Area is their favorite campground. The lake is big enough for skiing and there is no limit on boat or motor size.

FAIRFIELD LAKE STATE RECREATION AREA

6 miles northeast of Fairfield off F.M. 1124 in Freestone County, 90 miles southeast of Dallas.
Entrance fee: $2 per car

This is a fairly large park. The lake was created in 1969 when Texas Electric Utilities dammed Big Brown Creek to get cooling water for a power plant. The power plant uses the local lignite for fuel. It is on the opposite side of the lake from the park. The lake covers 2,400 acres. The park is 1,460 acres. Part of it is grassy prairie and part of it is shaded by oak and hickory trees. There are dogwood trees, too, and lots of wildflowers in the spring.

A variety of waterfowl can be seen here, including geese, great blue herons and double-crested cormorants. Fishermen get large-mouth bass, crappie, catfish, bluegill and drum here. The park has two double boat ramps with docks, fish-cleaning tables and a lighted fishing pier. The fishing probably is what interests most visitors. A park store operated by a concessionaire has boats for rent and some camping and picnic supplies.

The park has a swimming beach with no lifeguards, four playgrounds and an amphitheater. Visitors interested in hiking and primitive camping will find a parking area just inside the park entrance. A trail leads from here, across Big Brown Creek to a primitive camping area on the opposite side of the lake. The distance is three and one half miles. There are 12 campsites and a restroom. The campsites are $4 a night.

Campers looking for a few more comforts will find three camping areas on the east side of the lake. The Springfield Campground has 36 camp sites with water for $4 a night. The Cooks Ferry and Post Oak campgrounds have a total of 99

sites with water and electricity for $6 a night. The restrooms in the campgrounds all have showers. There are no screened shelters or cabins in this park. There is a picnic area near the swimming beach for day visitors.

For more information

You can make reservations or get more information about Fairfield Lake State Recreation Area by writing the Superintendent, Rt. 2, Box P-30, Fairfield, TX 75840 or by calling (214) 389-4514.

Other places to see

Several places to see nearby are Fort Parker State Recreation Area, 20 miles southwest on State Highway 14, 6 miles south of Mexia; Old Fort Parker State Historic Site, 25 miles southwest on State Highway 14, 11 miles south of Mexia; and Confederate Reunion Grounds, 20 miles southwest on F.M. 1633, 6 miles southwest of Mexia.

Top: A few of the campsites in the Fairfield Lake State Recreation Area are right on the lake so campers can keep their boats handy. These are the sites most in demand here.

Opposite: The Fort Parker State Recreation Area is a few miles south of a town with a name strangers sometimes have trouble with. Mexia is Spanish. Not all Spanish names in Texas take Spanish pronunciations. This one does. It is *mu-HAY-uh*.

FORT PARKER STATE RECREATION AREA

6 miles south of Mexia off State Highway 14 in Limestone County, 90 miles south of Dallas.
Entrance fee: $2 per car

This is one of the CCC parks, established in the 1930s. The dam on the Navasota River, built by the men of the CCC, created a lake of 750 acres. The park is 735 acres surrounding the lake. The land was donated to the state by the city of Mexia and three individual property owners in 1935 and 1936.

Fishing is the biggest attraction here, but skiing is also popular. Most of the park is heavily wooded and deeply shaded. Most of the trees are oak. White-tail deer, grey foxes, cotton-tail rabbits and many squirrels live in the deep woods. The park and lake attract a variety of birds also. Red-tailed hawks, barred owls, belted kingfishers, red-bellied woodpeckers, eastern phoebes and lake sparrows live here. Ospreys, yellow-billed cuckoos, winter wrens, orchard orioles and summer tanagers are some of the species migrating through here.

The fish caught here are mostly crappie, large-mouth bass, catfish and sunfish. There are fishing piers, a boat ramp and docks and a fish-cleaning table. A park store operated by a concessionaire sells bait and rents fishing boats.

One of the early towns in Limestone County was here on the Navasota River where the park is today. The town of Springfield was established in 1844. It had 400 people at its peak and was the county seat for Limestone County until 1873. The Houston and Texas Central Railroad passed Springfield by. A new town called Groesbeck grew up on the rail line. The county government and most of the population of Springfield moved to Groesbeck. The old townsite is largely under water now. The Springfield Cemetery is in the park on the east bank of the lake. This lake is called Lake Springfield on some maps and Fort Parker Lake on others.

This park has a hiking trail and a wilderness camping area. There are 10 screened shelters for rent at $8 a night, 14 campsites with water and electricity at $6 a night and 13 sites with water at $4 a night. All these campsites have tables, benches and grills and each has its own parking space. The restrooms in the camping areas have showers and laundry tubs.

There are 70 individual picnic sites here and one picnic pavillion that is available free on the basis of first come, first served.

The park also has a group picnic shelter with 10 tables, benches and grills available at $50 a day. A group camp can accommodate up to 92 people. It has a large dining hall and kitchen complete with refrigerator and freezer. No utensils or dishes are furnished. This camp has four dormitories and two restrooms. It is on the water near the old Springfield Cemetery. It is $100 a night. No bedding or linens are furnished.

This park takes its name from a stockade a family named Parker built near here in the 1830s. (See Old Fort Parker State Historic Site.)

For more information

More information about this park can be obtained by writing to the Superintendent, Rt. 3, Box 95, Mexia, TX 76667 or by calling (817) 562-5751.

Other places to see

Close by are Old Fort Parker State Historic Site, 5 miles farther south on State Highway 14 and Fairfield Lake State Recreation Area, 20 miles northeast off F.M. 1124, just 6 miles northeast of Fairfield. The park and the lake at Fairfield are bigger, but I think Fort Parker is more attractive.

The parks people have rebuilt old Fort Parker twice since the building the Parkers built fell down. This is a replica because there was not enough of the original left for a restoration. The replica was designed by restoration architect Raiford Stripling of San Augustine.

OLD FORT PARKER STATE HISTORIC SITE

Off State Highway 14, 11 miles south of Mexia in Limestone County, 95 miles south of Dallas. No entrance fee. Tour fees: adults $1, children 25¢

This is a replica of a family fort built by Elder John Parker and some of his relatives and friends in 1834. Eight or nine families were living here in 1836 when a band of Comanches attacked. The Indians killed Elder John Parker and four others and kidnapped several of the survivors. Elder John Parker's granddaughter, Cynthia Ann, was one of those kidnapped. She was 9 years old at the time.

The Comanches raised Cynthia Ann as an Indian and in time she forgot she was not an Indian. A Comanche chief named Peta Nocona took her as one of his wives. They had several children. Cynthia Ann had one of the children with her when Texas Rangers recaptured her in north Texas in 1860. The child was a girl, just 2 years old, and she was called Prairie Flower. She died about three years after she and her mother were returned to the Parker family. Cynthia Ann died a short time later. People thought it was because she never adjusted to the loss of her Indian family.

Cynthia Ann Parker's story attracted a great deal of public notice at the time and it has received a lot of attention ever since because one of the sons she had by Peta Nocona grew up to become the great chief of the Quahadi Comanches. He led his people in their last stand against the U.S. Army in the Texas Panhandle and became an Indian elder statesman and media celebrity after he gave up

the fight. Cynthia Ann Parker and Prairie Flower were buried in Anderson County. Their remains were moved to Oklahoma and reinterred beside Quanah Parker's grave after he died in 1911.

The Parker fort disintegrated long years before Texans started getting interested in such relics. A replica was built here during the Texas Centennial celebration in 1936. It disintegrated, too. The present replica was built in 1967 with cedar logs from the Buescher State Park at Smithville. It is in good shape and seems likely to last for many more years. It is believed to be on the site of the original Parker fort.

The Parkers were from Illinois. They patterned their stockade after those the settlers in the northeastern United States had built earlier, with blockhouses at two corners where defenders could fire down on anyone trying to force the gate or climb the walls.

There is no entrance fee to the park, but there is a charge of $1 for adults and 25 cents for children for the tour of the stockade. An annual pass or a senior citizen's passport is good for the admission fee. Visitors guide themselves on this tour. Signs around the compound explain the various features. Children enjoy climbing into the blockhouses and staging mock battles. Special guided tours can be arranged and there is a special rate for student groups.

For more information

The phone number for more information is (817) 729-5253. The mailing address is Old Fort Parker Historic Site, Rt. 3, Box 220, Groesbeck, TX 76642.

Other places to see

Other state parks in this area are Fort Parker State Recreation Area, 5 miles north on State Highway 14; and Fairfield Lake State Recreation Area, 25 miles northeast off F.M. 1124, 6 miles northeast of Fairfield. Both have campgrounds.

The Joseph E. Johnson Camp No. 94 of the Confederate Veterans maintained this camp with the help of oilman A. E. Humphries before it became the Confederate Reunion Grounds State Historical Park in 1984.

CONFEDERATE REUNION GROUNDS STATE HISTORICAL PARK

6 miles southwest of Mexia at junction of F.M. 2705 and F.M. 1633 in Limestone County, 90 miles south of Dallas.
No entrance fee

Confederate veterans of the Civil War established this park in 1892. Veterans from all over central Texas used to meet here every summer and their descendants have continued the custom. The park was privately maintained until 1984 when it was deeded to the Parks and Wildlife Department by Confederate Veterans Joe Johnson Camp No. 94. The department is still working on improvements. The park is open for picnicking in the meantime. It is on the Navasota River, just upstream from Fort Parker State Recreation Area.

This park covers 75 wooded acres. There are hiking trails, a playground, restrooms, several picnic sites and two pavillions. There is no entrance fee. The park is open only from 8 a.m. to 5 p.m.

For more information

Requests for information about the Confederate Reunion Grounds are being handled for the time being by the Superintendent of Fort Parker State Recreation Area, Rt. 3, Box 95, Mexia, TX 76667; telephone, (817) 562-5751.

Other places to see

Fort Parker State Recreation Area and campgrounds is 6 miles south of Mexia on State Highway 14. Old Fort Parker State Historic Site is 11 miles south of Mexia off State Highway 14.

1. San Jacinto Battleground Historical Park
2. Battleship Texas Historic Site
3. Galveston Island State Park
4. Bryan Beach State Recreation Area
5. Varner-Hogg Historical Park
6. Brazos Bend State Park
7. Stephen F. Austin Historical Park
8. Washington-on-the-Brazos Historical Park
9. Lake Somerville State Recreation Area
10. Huntsville State Park
11. Lake Livingston State Recreation Area
12. Cassells Boykin State Park
13. Martin Dies Jr. State Park
14. Sabine Pass Battleground Historical Park
15. Sea Rim State Park

REGION IV
PARKS IN SOUTHEAST TEXAS

There are 15 state parks, recreation areas, historical parks and historic sites in southeast Texas. There will be 21 when the Texas Parks and Wildlife Department completes development of the five additional properties already bought. The principal city in this part of the state is Houston. The parks in this section are numbered as you would encounter them starting from Houston and traveling around the area clockwise. The numbers are not rankings. I would make Martin Dies Jr. State Park on Lake B. A. Steinhagen number one if I were ranking them.

Parks Under Development

There are four parks and one historical structure in various stages of development in this region.

Davis Hill Park, near Moss Hill in Liberty County. This is one of the old salt domes in the Big Thicket.

Lake Houston Park, in Harris and Montgomery counties off F.M. 1483, on the north side of the lake the San Jacinto River Authority and the city of Houston built in 1954. The site is 4,700 acres. The Parks and Wildlife Department bought it in 1981 for about $13.5 million. This is the biggest price the department has ever paid for a park site.

Sheldon Wildlife Management Area and State Park on Fauna Road, just north of old U.S. 90, 16 miles east of downtown Houston. This is the old Sheldon Reservoir and the land surrounding it. It has been a wildlife management area and refuge for years. The Parks and Wildlife Department started in the fall of 1984 to develop it as a state park.

Village Creek Park near Lumberton in Hardin County in the Big Thicket. The site is approximately 950 acres. The Parks and Wildlife Department paid about $900,000 for it in 1980.

The historic Fanthorp Inn, at Anderson, in Grimes County, was started by Henry Fanthorp in colonial days. The Parks and Wildlife Department bought the building and grounds in 1977 for about $100,000. At present, there are no plans for a full restoration. The building is being repaired and stabilized and it may be open to the public by the end of 1985. There are several other interesting old buildings in Anderson, including the quaintest courthouse in Texas.

SAN JACINTO BATTLEGROUND HISTORICAL PARK

State Highway 134 off State 225 in southeast Harris County, 22 miles east of downtown Houston. No entrance fee

About one and one-half million people visit the San Jacinto Battleground every year. The biggest day for visitors, usually, is April 21. This is the anniversary of the battle that ended the Texas Revolution and established Texas independence.

A widow named Peggy McCormick operated a farm here in 1836. The location was of some consequence because Nathaniel Lynch had established a ferry nearby in 1831 to carry traffic across the junction of the San Jacinto River and Buffalo Bayou. The road to the ferry landing was an important road. Many settlers fleeing from Santa Anna's Mexican army were using this road. This is one of the reasons Santa Anna came here. The Mexican leader was enjoying a little recreation in his tent with a local girl he had just met when Sam Houston's Texas Army attacked the Mexican camp here the afternoon of April 21, 1836. It was a brief battle. The Texans lost only eight men. They killed about 650 Mexicans and captured hundreds more.

Santa Anna was captured the day after the battle as he was trying to slip away to Richmond where he had 2,000 more troops. A stone marker stands near the water's edge at the site where the victorious Sam Houston and the captured Mexican president first met. The Daughters of the Republic of Texas have put up stone markers around the battleground where various Texas and Mexican units were camped and where some of the more important events of that eventful day occur-

Markers around the San Jacinto Battleground State Historical Park explain who was here and some of what happened in April, 1836. There is a historical museum in the base of the monument in the background.

red. The Texans were camped near the approach to Lynch's ferry landing. (The ferry is still operating. It is called the Lynchburg Ferry now and is maintained by Harris County.) The Mexicans were camped on the opposite side of the San Jacinto Monument. The reflection pool is approximately on the ground the Texans covered during their surprise advance that afternoon. The monument is about where the heaviest fighting occurred.

The San Jacinto Monument is one of the tallest masonry monuments in the world. It is 570 feet tall with an observation deck on top. The fee for riding the elevator to the observation deck is $1.50 for adults and 50 cents for children under 12. There is no charge for admission to the park or to the museum in the base of the monument. The park and museum are open seven days a week from 10 a.m. to 6 p.m. The federal government paid most of the cost of the San Jacinto Monument. It was one of the Roosevelt Administration's WPA projects. Work started during the Texas Centennial celebration in 1936. It was finished in 1939.

There are 83 picnic sites around the battleground. Camping is not permitted.

For more information

You can get more information about the battleground and museum from San Jacinto Battleground Park, 3523 Highway 134, La Porte, TX 77571 or San Jacinto Museum, 3800 Park Road 1836, La Porte, TX 77571. The phone number for the park is (713) 479-2431. The museum number is (713) 479-2019.

Other places to see

There are many attractions in the area including the city of Houston, the Astrodome, the Lyndon B. Johnson Manned Spacecraft Center on NASA Road 1 and Galveston Island State Park on F.M. 3005 on West Galveston Island.

BATTLESHIP TEXAS STATE HISTORIC SITE

At San Jacinto Battleground on State Highway 134 off State Highway 225 in southeast Harris County, 22 miles east of downtown Houston.
Fees: adults $3, children $1

This is the second U.S. warship to be named for this state. The first one was commissioned in 1892 and took part in a few engagements during the Spanish American War. This ship was commissioned in 1914. It served in the Atlantic during World War I and in both the Atlantic and the Pacific during World War II. It has been berthed here at the San Jacinto Battleground since San Jacinto Day, 1948. It has been a unit of the state park system since 1983.

The *Texas* launched the first airplane ever launched from a naval vessel. That was in 1919. The engine in the *Texas* is said to be the last steam piston engine in the world. There is a museum on board and visitors can see a film about the battleship.

The *Texas* is open to visitors every day, 10 a.m. to 5 p.m. in the winter and 10 a.m. to 6 p.m. in the summer. The admission fees are $3 for adults, $1 for children. Senior citizens can get in for $2. There is no charge for children under 6 and school groups can get a special rate.

For more information

You can write to Battleship *Texas,* 3527 Battleground Road, La Porte, TX 77571, or phone (713) 479-2411 if you need more information about the battleship.

Other places to see

Other interesting places close by are the Battleground and Museum, the Lyndon B. Johnson Manned Spacecraft Center on NASA Road 1, Galveston Island State Park on F.M. 3005, Houston and the Astrodome.

The old battleship *Texas* has been docked at the San Jacinto Battleground and open for visitors since 1948. There is a special visitor's book for former members of the warship's crew. A number of them have visited here.

GALVESTON ISLAND STATE PARK

On F.M. 3005, West Galveston Island, 60 miles southeast of Houston. Entrance fee: $2 per car

Galveston Island State Park extends from the Gulf of Mexico to Galveston Bay. It includes more than one and one-half miles of beach on the Gulf side and acres of swamp and marshland on the bay side. The park straddles F.M. 3005, 6 miles beyond the end of the Galveston seawall. It is one of the most popular parks in the state system.

This was a cattle ranch until 1970. It had been owned by Maco Stewart. He was one of the founders of the Stewart Title Company. It was Stewart's idea that the ranch should be a state park. He left the ranch to the state when he died, but he left a life interest to his heirs. The Parks and Wildlife Department bought the heirs' life interest in June, 1970, for $890,875 and started developing the park. Texans are the biggest users of the park in the summer. Visitors from the North make heavy use of it in the fall and winter. The campground is open the year round.

There are some nature trails with picnic sites and blinds for birdwatchers on the bay side of the park. Bird checklists are available at park headquarters. Birdwatchers and hikers should be aware that rattlesnakes are not uncommon here.

Most of the picnic sites and campsites in this park are concentrated on the beach side right behind where the dunes were until Alicia washed most of the dunes away in August, 1983. Each of the 60 picnic sites has a shade shelter, picnic table and a grill. There is no charge for the picnic shelters beyond the park admission fee and the picnic sites cannot be reserved. There are 150 campsites on the beach side with water, electricity, shade shelter, table and grill for $6 a night. The public restrooms in the camping and picnic areas have showers.

Galveston Island State Park has 10 screened shelters on the bay side overlooking an inlet called Lake Como. These have electricity, water, table and grill. They are $8 a night. There are showers in the public restroom nearby. Also nearby is a group trailer camp with 20 campsites equipped with water and electricity. These are $6 a night.

The park has a couple of small fresh water lakes. Salt-water fishermen get flounder, trout and red drum here. *Texas Fisherman* editor Larry Bozka says the surf fishing here is best from early spring to mid-summer, when the wind is in the southeast. He says live shrimp under a popping cork will produce speckled trout and a variety of panfish.

The first European came to Galveston Island in 1520, by accident. He was Cabeza de Vaca and he was shipwrecked. He left as soon as he could. One of the early residents was the privateer Jean Laffite. He was here between 1817 and 1821 while Texas was still claimed by Spain. The city of Galveston was established right after the Texas Revolution. It was the biggest, richest and most important city in Texas for more than 50 years. Many of the buildings built during Galveston's heyday are still standing. Some have been restored and some are open to visitors. You can get information about these from the Galveston Historical Foundation on The Strand in downtown Galveston. The phone number is (409) 765-7834.

The Mary Moody Northen Amphitheater on the eastern edge of Galveston Island State Park is one of the most elaborate outdoor theaters in the country. It is named for Mrs. Northen because she gave the money to build it. Mrs. Northen inherited part of the great fortune accumulated by her father and grandfather. They were the pioneer cotton brokers, bankers and insurers, W. L. Moody and W. L. Moody, Jr.

The amphitheater puts on musical shows every night during the summer. One of the shows was written for this theater by Paul Green. It is called *Lone Star* and it is based on the Texas Revolution. Another musical is presented on alternate nights. *Annie Get Your Gun* ran for several summers. *Hello, Dolly* became the alternate show in 1984. The show's casts are made up of college students and some professional actors. They live in the theater complex during the summer. The theater complex also includes a Western cafeteria where theatergoers can have a chuck wagon dinner before the show. Dinner is served between 6 and 8 p.m. Prices the last time we checked were $4.95 for adults and $3 for children. General admission tickets for the shows are $5 for adults and $3 for children. Reserved seats are $6 and $7 for adults and $4 for children. The shows are well done. The dinners run mostly to chicken fried steak and fish.

For more information

For more information about Galveston Island State Park and for reservations, write Rt. 1, Box 156A, Galveston, TX 77551. The phone number is (409) 737-1222.

Other places to see

This area is full of attractions worth seeing. Some are the Lyndon B. Johnson Manned Spacecraft Center on NASA Road 1 off I-45 about 25 miles north of Galveston, San Jacinto Battleground State Historical Park on State Highway 134 off State Highway 225 in southeast Harris County, the Battleship *Texas* at the battleground, the restoration and renovation work on The Strand and Mechanic Street in downtown Galveston, the Museum of Transportation in the old Santa Fe Building at 25th and The Strand downtown, the new San Luis Hotel at Old Fort Crockett on the Seawall and the Balinese Room on the Seawall at 22nd Street (a plush gambling resort in the 1930s and 40s). A tour train operates from the Convention Center across from the Galvez Hotel at 22nd and Seawall. A submarine and a destroyer from World War II are on display at Seawolf Park on Pelican Island, where there once was a quarantine station for immigrants. A free ferry runs from the east end of Galveston Island to Bolivar Peninsula. The access road off the Seawall just east of Stewart Beach is well marked.

Top: The picnic areas in Galveston Island State Park are crowded with Texans in the summer and the camping areas are filled in the winter with people from colder climates.

Bottom: Galveston Island State Park has more than a mile and a half of beach. Some Texans think they have a constitutional right to drive their vehicles on the beach. They cannot do it here.

BRYAN BEACH STATE RECREATION AREA

Off County Road 723 outside Freeport in Brazoria County 62 miles south of Houston. No fees

Bryan Beach State Park is an undeveloped stretch of beach that may be a park some day, or it may not. The site is bordered on the north by the Intracoastal Canal. The Corps of Engineers dumps some of the spoil dredged out of the canal adjacent to the park site. The spoil does not add anything to the attractiveness of the site. The Parks and Wildlife Department appears in no rush to do any developing, after spending more than $1 million to acquire this 878 acres in the 1970s.

There is nothing to prevent people from camping on the park site and people do camp here. There is no fee and no one to collect any fees.

The history of Bryan Beach is more distinguished than its present. The beach took its name from James Perry Bryan. He built a home here about 1881 and raised his family here while he was operating a store at Peach Point. The Bryans were some of the earliest settlers in Brazoria County. James Perry Bryan's grandmother was Stephen F. Austin's sister.

For more information

Inquiries about Bryan Beach State Park are handled by the staff at Galveston Island State Park, Rt. 1, Box 156A, Galveston, TX 77551. The telephone number is (409) 737-1222.

VARNER-HOGG STATE HISTORICAL PARK

On Park Road 51 off State Highway 35, just east of West Columbia in Brazoria County, 58 miles south of Houston. No entrance fee. Tour fees: adults $1, children 25¢

The Varner-Hogg State Historical Park was donated to the Parks and Wildlife Department in 1956 by the late Ima Hogg. Her father was Gov. Jim Hogg. He had bought this property and the surrounding plantation in 1901 after he left the governor's office. Ima and her brothers, Will, Mike and Tom, spent part of their childhood here. They improved and remodeled the house after oil was discovered on the property in 1920. The Hoggs used the house as a weekend retreat for many years and entertained many important people here. Ima Hogg filled the house with fine furniture and antiques and gave all the furnishings to the Parks and Wildlife Department when she deeded the house and grounds to the state.

The original owner of this plantation was Martin Varner. He was one of the original 300 settlers in the Stephen F. Austin colony. Varner was granted 4,605 acres on the stream that has been called Varner Creek ever since he settled here in 1824. Martin Varner raised sugar cane and made a little rum before he sold the plantation to Columbus Patton in 1834. The Pattons raised sugar, cotton and corn here until Columbus died in 1856. The plantation went through several changes in ownership before Jim Hogg bought it. Hogg was practicing law in Houston and speculating in oil lands when he moved his family here. He told his family he believed there was oil on the plantation, but it was not discovered in his lifetime. He died in 1906.

The main house here is thought to have been built by the Pattons in the 1830s. It was a sturdy and comfortable house in their time, but the house today is not the house the Pattons knew. This is not a restoration. It is an early Texas plantation house remodeled and redecorated by a very rich woman with considerable taste. It really is a museum and the staff conducting the tours tell many stories

Bryan Beach Park is more beach than park. There are no improvements. There is no fee.

about the Hoggs and their interests. Some of them knew Ima Hogg. She visited here often before she died in 1975.

There is no fee for admission to the grounds here and no camping. There are some picnic tables, but most visitors come here to see the house and furnishings. The fee for the tour of the house is $1 for adults and 25 cents for children. Tours are conducted on Tuesdays, Thursdays, Fridays and Saturdays from 10 a.m. to 11:30 a.m. and from 1 p.m. to 4:30 p.m. Tours are conducted on Sundays only from 1 p.m. to 4:30 p.m.

For more information

You can get more information or arrange for group tours by calling (409) 345-4656 or writing to Varner-Hogg Park, Box 696, West Columbia, TX 77486.

Other places to see

Other places to see in this area are East Columbia on the west bank of the Brazos River just off State Highway 35, a colonial river port originally known as Bell's Landing; West Columbia, where there is a replica of the little building the first Congress of the Republic of Texas met in; and Brazos Bend State Park off F.M. 762 east of Damon in southeastern Fort Bend County.

Top: Stephen F. Austin said he thought the rum that Martin Varner made on this plantation in 1829 was the first strong drink produced in Texas. The present house at the Varner-Hogg Plantation was built by the second owner, Columbus Patton.

Opposite: The Parks and Wildlife Department has built an observation platform on one of the little lakes in this park so visitors can observe the birds and alligators.

BRAZOS BEND STATE PARK

Off F.M. 762, east of Damon in Fort Bend County, 67 miles south of Houston. Entrance fee: $2 per car

Brazos Bend is a very large park and one of the newer ones. The lands here in the lower Brazos valley were the first to be occupied by the colonists Stephen F. Austin brought into Texas in the early 1820s. The land that is now park was granted originally to Abner Harris and William Barrett. The last private owners were Herman and Nancy Hale of Houston. They used it for grazing cattle and as a private hunting preserve. The Parks and Wildlife Department bought it in 1977.

The site has three and a half miles of river frontage and several small lakes.

Hurricane Alicia blew down a number of big trees here in August, 1983, and the damage delayed the opening of Brazos Bend State Park until early 1984. Plenty of trees are left. They are mostly oak, elm and pecan with sycamore and cottonwood along the river. This is a great place for birdwatchers, especially in the fall when the ducks and other migratory birds are here. The rangers say more than 200 species have been sighted here. The department has built an observation tower on one of the small lakes for visitors interested in spying on the birds and wildlife. Visitors are quite likely to see white-tail deer and they may see a bobcat, raccoon, possum, grey fox, coyote, Russian boar or a feral hog. No one has attempted to count the alligators in the lakes here.

Brazos Bend State Park covers almost 5,000 acres and only about half of this area is accessible by car. Most of the development has been around the lakes. There are fishing piers, but swimming and boating are prohibited. There is nothing along the river except a hiking trail. This trail is three miles long. The park has another 12 miles of trails, including a hike-and-bike trail.

Three picnic areas in the park have a total of 120 picnic sites. The primitive camping area has 20 sites at $4 a night. The tent camping area has 35 sites at $4 a night. A trailer camping area has 42 sites with electricity at $6 a night. There are 14 screened shelters for rent at $8 a night. Restrooms in the camping areas have showers, except in the primitive camping area.

The park has a group dining hall. Reservations are required for it and they are advisable for anyone planning to stay overnight. The park has become very popular in the short time it has been open.

For more information

You can write to Brazos Bend Park, Rt. 1, Box 840, Needville, TX 77461, or call (409) 553-3243 to make a reservation or get more information about this park.

Other places to see

Other places you might want to see in this area are Varner-Hogg State Historical Park off State Highway 35 just east of West Columbia; the replica of the hall where the first Congress of the Republic of Texas met in 1836 just off Highway 35 in downtown West Columbia; and the little town of East Columbia just off Highway 35 at the Brazos River, originally known as Bell's Landing. Both East Columbia and West Columbia go back to colonial times and East Columbia looks it.

Left: There are fishing piers on the lakes in Brazos Bend State Park, but no boats are allowed and no swimming is permitted. The lakes are infested with alligators.

Opposite: The swimming pool at Stephen F. Austin State Historical Park is popular with campers and day visitors, too. It is open only during the summer months. The campgrounds are open the year round.

STEPHEN F. AUSTIN STATE HISTORICAL PARK

Out of San Felipe off F.M. 1458, just north of I-10, just east of Sealy in Austin County, 52 miles west of Houston. Entrance fee: $2 per car

San Felipe was an important town in colonial Texas. The original Anglo empressario, Stephen F. Austin, had his headquarters here. The county is named for him. San Felipe began to decline after the county government moved from here to Bellville in 1846. The present town occupies only a fraction of the original townsite, but about six historic buildings remain. None is in the park, but most of the park was part of the original townsite. It was given to the state by the town of San Felipe in 1940.

One of the important roads in Texas in colonial days was the Atascocita Road between Goliad and southeast Texas. The Atascocita Road crossed the Brazos here. This is why Stephen F. Austin chose this site for his headquarters. There was a ferry across the river then and the cut in the riverbank, leading down to the ferry landing, is still visible here beside the F.M. 1458 bridge. The center of the old town of San Felipe was here beside the ferry landing. Twelve acres, straddling F.M. 1458, on the south side of the river are maintained as a historic site. There is a monument and statue of Stephen F. Austin, the original town well, an early general store building and museum, a log cabin that may be similar to the one Stephen F. Austin lived in and some picnic tables in this section of the park. There is no admission fee for this part of the park except a small fee for

the museum. The usual fee is required for admission to the park proper.

The main unit of Stephen F. Austin State Historical Park is on Park Road 38 a short distance west of the historic site. The 650 acres here are almost covered with large oak trees. Spanish moss helps make the site picturesque. Most of the campsites have deep shade, but they get pretty warm in midsummer because there is not a lot of air circulating. This park has 40 tent campsites for $4 a night and 40 trailer camping sites with hookups for $7 a night. Twenty screened shelters with water, electricity, tables and grills are available at $8 a night. The public restrooms in the camping areas have hot showers. There is one large group shelter with a kitchen available for day use only at $50 a day. This park is very popular with Scouts and other youth groups. There are two playgrounds, a swimming pool and a golf course. The pool fees are $1 for adults and 50 cents for children. There are lifeguards.

The golf course at Stephen F. Austin State Historical Park is the only 18-hole course in the state park system. It is operated by the Stephen F. Austin Golf Association. The greens fees are $7 on weekdays and $14 on weekends and holidays. Golf carts are available for $12.

The Brazos makes a bend here and the river forms the northern and eastern boundaries of the park. There is no fishing pier, but some visitors do fish the river from the bank.

For more information

You can make reservations or get more information about Stephen F. Austin State Historical Park by writing the Superintendent at Box 125, San Felipe, TX 77473 or calling (409) 885-3613. The golf course number is (409) 885-2811.

Other places to see

While you are in this area, you may want to see the historic buildings in Columbus (you can get information and a map for a walking tour from the Chamber of Commerce office in the old Opera House on the courthouse square), Fayetteville and Bellville. Take F.M. 1094 from Sealy to New Ulm, F.M. 109 from New Ulm to Frelsburg, F.M. 1291 from Frelsburg to Fayetteville, State Highway 159 from Fayetteville through Industry to Bellville and State Highway 36 from Bellville back to Sealy, especially if you are here in the wildflower season.

The Republic of Texas existed for nine years. It started and ended at Washington-on-the-Brazos. The Declaration of Independence was signed here. The Constitution was written here. The ceremony marking the annexation to the United States was held here. Dr. Anson Jones was the last president of the republic. He built this home on his plantation a few miles from here. It was moved to the park in 1936.

WASHINGTON-ON-THE-BRAZOS STATE HISTORICAL PARK

On F.M. 1155 off State Highway 105 about 7 miles southwest of Navasota in Washington County, 82 miles northwest of Houston. No entrance fee

Washington-on-the-Brazos State Historical Park occupies most of the site of the old town of Washington. Little is left of the town itself, but Washington was the last capital of the Republic of Texas. The Texas Declaration of Independence was signed here on March 2, 1836.

La Bahia Road between Goliad and East Texas crossed the Brazos River here in colonial days. A settler named Andrew Robinson started a ferry here in 1822 to serve the immigrants and travelers and to make a little money. John Hall started the town in 1835. He had married Robinson's daughter. Most of the other important meetings the settlers held during the Mexican rule were in San Felipe, but the Convention of 1836 was held in Washington because some local people offered a hall. It was not much of a hall and it disappeared many years ago, but what the delegates to the Convention of 1836 did in the hall had a profound effect upon the history of North America.

The government of the republic took office at Columbia, where West Columbia is today. It moved from there to Houston and then to Austin. The government moved from Austin to Washington during Sam Houston's second term as president. Dr. Anson Jones succeeded Houston as president and Jones built a home just outside Washington. Jones presided here at the ceremoney marking Texas' entry into the Union in 1845. The state government made Austin its capital and the county government moved to Brenham, but Washington continued to prosper as a river port and trading center into the 1850s. The prosperity declined abruptly when the railroad era began because Washington's leaders declined to offer the railroads any inducements to put a line here.

The population of Washington dropped from about 4,000 in 1860 to about 200

in 1885. Buildings were abandoned to fall down or be torn down. The legislature appropriated money in 1916 to buy about 50 acres of the old townsite. The hall where the Declaration of Independence was signed was already gone. The state built a replica of the hall and an auditorium and named the site Washington Park.

The 100th anniversary of independence in 1936 raised interest in historic sites to a new high. The state bought more land for Washington Park, built an amphitheater and moved to the park the home Anson Jones had built at his Barrington Plantation. Little more happened though until some local people in 1955 formed the Texas Independence Day Organization to preserve and promote the park. This organization evolved into the Washington-on-the-Brazos State Park Association. This association raised money to help pay for some of the improvements that are here today — the Star of the Republic Museum and a better replica of Independence Hall on the exact site where the original stood. The Barrington Historical Society helped restore and furnish the Anson Jones house. The Parks and Wildlife Department had a lot of help in making this park a suitable memorial to the signers of the Texas Declaration of Independence. George Butler and Jim Ethridge were two of the leaders of the Washington-on-the-Brazos State Park Association.

The park now covers 154 acres. There is a pleasant picnic area and playground, but no provision for camping. The park is open from 8 a.m. till sundown every day. There is no entrance fee. The fee for the conducted tours of the Anson Jones house is $1 for adults and 50 cents for children. The auditorium can be rented for meetings and reunions and the like for $55, or $70 with the kitchen. There is no fee for using the amphitheater. The Star of the Republic Museum is staffed by Blinn College of Brenham. It is free.

For more information

You can get more information by writing the Superintendent at Box 305, Washington, TX 77880 or by calling (409) 878-2214.

Other places to see

Other places of interest in this area are Independence (where Baylor University started), west on F.M. 390; Brenham (the Bluebell Ice Cream plant conducts tours), south on U.S. 290; Chappell Hill (several historic buildings), south on U.S. 290; and Anderson (numerous historic buildings, one of the quaintest courthouses in Texas, and the Fanthorp Inn, being restored as a State Historic Site), northeast on State Highway 90. The best time to visit this area is during bluebonnet season.

The group picnic shelter in the Nails Creek Unit of Lake Somerville State Recreation Area. This area is carpeted with wildflowers in the spring. Visitors are apt to see whitetail deer, armadillos and rabbits here and they may see an occasional fox, coyote, raccoon or possum.

LAKE SOMERVILLE STATE RECREATION AREA

Northwest of Brenham off State Highway 36 in Burleson and Lee counties, 85 miles northwest of Houston. Entrance fee: $2 per car

President Reagan probably would be partial to this park if he knew about it. It is one of the few parks in the system with special provisions for visitors with horses. The hiking trail in this park is the longest trail in the system. It is 21 miles long and it is open to hikers, bicyclists and horseback riders. There are special camping areas for riders at each end of the trail and parking areas for their trailers.

The Somerville park is in two units on opposite sides of Lake Somerville. The lake was created to help control flooding in the Brazos River watershed. There are 640 acres in the Birch Creek Unit on the north shore and 300 acres in the Nails Creek Unit on the south shore. The hike-bike-horse trail runs around the upper end of the lake. There are five camping areas along this trail, with water and toilets. The equestrian campground in the Birch Creek Unit has 20 sites. The equestrian camp at Nails Creek has 10 sites, without electricity.

There are 103 campsites with water and electricity in the Birch Creek Unit for $6 a night. The restrooms in the camping areas have showers. There are boat ramps, docks and fish-cleaning tables.

The Nails Creek Unit has 40 campsites with water and electricity at $6 a night. This lake is popular with skiers, but the state park is near the upper end of the lake. The Nails Creek Unit, especially, is far enough from the dam to be almost without water when the lake level is low. You may want to try the Corps of

Engineers parks in such times. The Corps maintains five parks near the dam. All of them have more water than the state park. Some of them have campgrounds and picnic tables and boat ramps. Some are operated by the corps and some by concessionaires. All of them can be reached from State Highway 36. The Corps of Engineers controls all the land around this lake. The two units of the Lake Somerville State Recreation Area are on land the state leases from the Corps.

For more information

To make reservations or get more information about the Birch Creek Unit, write to the Superintendent, Rt. 1, Box 499, Somerville, TX 77879 or call (409) 535-7763. The address of the Nails Creek Unit is Rt. 1, Box 61C, Ledbetter, TX 78946. The phone there is (409) 289-2392.

You can address inquiries about the Corps of Engineers parks to the Reservoir Manager, P.O. Box 548, Somerville, TX 77879; phone, (409) 596-1622.

Other places to see

Other places of interest in this area are College Station (Texas A&M), 25 miles northeast on F.M. 60; Independence (first home of Baylor University and one of the places Sam Houston lived), 20 miles east on F.M. 390; Washington-on-the-Brazos State Historical Park (where the Texas Declaration of Independence was signed), about 35 miles east off State Highway 105 and Brenham (several historic buildings and the Blue Bell Ice Cream Plant), about 20 miles southeast on State Highway 36.

A small part of the small lake in Huntsville State Park is roped off and reserved for swimming.

HUNTSVILLE STATE PARK

On Park Road 40 just west of I-45, just south of Huntsville in Walker County, 69 miles north of Houston. Entrance fee: $2 per car

Huntsville State Park is one of our older parks and it must be a substantially prettier place today than it was when it was established in the middle 1930s.

The original Texas pine forests were cut down by the lumber companies between 1880 and 1930. There was not much forest left here when the Gibbs Brothers Company and W. B. Fraser donated this 2,100 acres to the Texas State Parks Board in 1934. The second growth of trees has reached impressive size now and the average visitor does not guess that it is second growth.

Huntsville State Park is in the northwest corner of the Sam Houston National Forest. The trees are loblolly and short-leaf pine, sweetgum, red maple and oak. There is plenty of dogwood, too; so the park is at its prettiest in late March and early April. The hardwoods are colorful in the fall. There are deer and lots of birds.

The CCC built the original improvements here. The parks the CCC built in Texas are similar but different. Most have a lake and a shelter or bathhouse and some have boathouses. Several have stone terraces on the waterfront similar to the one here. The styles vary from park to park, but you will be able to spot a CCC park after you have seen a few.

The lake here is just a little over 200 acres. Big boats and water skiiing are

not allowed. The concessionaire rents small rowboats, canoes and pedal boats. You can bring your own boat if it is not more than 19 feet long and the motor is not bigger than 12 horsepower. There is a small swimming beach, but no lifeguard. You swim at your own risk. The park also has a boat ramp, two fishing piers, fish-cleaning tables, playground, miniature golf course, bicycle trail, nature trail and hiking trail. A group picnic shelter is available for day use for reunions and meetings. It is just $8 if there are no more than 25 in the party and $16 if the party is between 25 and 75 people.

The Coloneh Camping Area here has 127 campsites with water, grill and picnic table for $4 a night. *Coloneh* is the Cherokee word for Raven. It is the name the Cherokees gave Sam Houston when they admitted him to their tribe.

The Raven Hill Camping Area has 26 trailer camping sites with water, electricity, table and grill for $6 a night. The Prairie Branch Camping Area has 38 sites with electricity, water, table and grill for $6 a night.

The park has 30 screened shelters on the lake for $8 a night and 105 picnic sites.

This is a very pleasant and popular park. Some families have been camping at Huntsville State Park for three generations. It has most of the features campers and picnickers are looking for. But if you want to launch a big boat or pull water skiers, you will want to consider Livingston, Martin Dies or Caddo Lake.

For more information

You can make reservations or get more information about this park by writing to the Superintendent, P.O. Box 508, Huntsville, TX 77340 or by calling (409) 295-5644.

Other places to see

At this park, you are near the Sam Houston Memorial Park in Huntsville, including an excellent museum, two of the houses the Houston family lived in and an office Houston used. Sam Houston died in Huntsville in 1863, two years after he was removed from the governor's office for refusing to swear allegiance to the Confederacy. Lake Livingston State Recreation Area is also near. Take U.S. 190 east 43 miles to U.S. 59. Go south on 59 to F.M. 1988 and follow the park signs.

Many Texas fishermen consider this the best white bass lake in the state. *Texas Fisherman* editor Larry Bozka says the best spots are the old Highway 190 roadbed and the old river channel near Walker Lake.

LAKE LIVINGSTON STATE RECREATION AREA

Off F.M. 3126, southeast of Livingston in Polk County, 73 miles northeast of Houston. Entrance fee: $2 per car

Lake Livingston was created by the Trinity River Authority and the city of Houston to furnish water for Houston. The lake covers almost 85,000 acres. It was completed in 1969. The state acquired the 635 acres for this park in 1972 and 1973. About 175 acres were donated; the state bought the rest.

The park is on the east bank of the lake with two and a half miles of lake frontage. It has just about everything water sports enthusiasts need — three boat ramps, a marina with fuel and bait, fish-cleaning shelters and miles of open water for fishing and skiing. It also has a small swimming beach, a bathhouse and a swimming pool with lifeguards on duty. Access to the beach is included in the entrance fee. There is an additional fee of $1 for adults and 50 cents for children for use of the bathhouse and pool.

It is wise to make reservations in advance in any of the state parks and especially in the popular campgrounds like this one. Livingston has ten screened shelters right on the water for rent at $8 a night. There are 97 campsites with water and electricity for $6 a night. Some of these are on the water and some are not. There is a group trailer camp with 50 sites at $6 a night and a group shelter at the trailer campground available free to groups renting the group camp.

The restrooms in the camping areas have showers. Some of the 64 picnic sites are right on the water. The park also has playgrounds, an amphitheater and about four miles of hiking trails.

The land where the park is now was part of the great East Texas oak and pine forest before the timber companies moved in. Most of this area had been turned into a pine tree farm before the lake was built. The trees are second or third growth, but the state is allowing the forest to return to its natural state. It gets better every year. Most of the trees are loblolly pine, but there are oaks and elms along

the creeks. The woods are full of deer and raccoons. The preliminary bird checklist the office has available for birdwatchers lists 98 species likely to be spotted here.

Huntsville, Livingston and Martin Dies Jr. parks have several features in common — woods, lakes and good campgrounds. Livingston has the biggest lake.

For more information

You can make reservations or get more information about Lake Livingston State Recreation Area by writing to the Superintendent, Rt. 9, Box 1300, Livingston, TX 77351 or by calling (409) 365-2201.

Other places to see

Other nearby places of interest are Huntsville, about 50 miles west on U.S. 190 (Huntsville State Park and Sam Houston Memorial Park); the Alabama-Coushatta Indian Reservation about 15 miles east on U.S. 190 (the Indians have an outdoor theater where they present a historical drama on summer nights and a pleasant campground for palefaces interested in spending a few days on the reservation); and Woodville (Allan Shivers Library and Museum and Heritage Garden).

Top: The swimming beach at Lake Livingston State Recreation Area is adjacent to the bathhouse and swimming pool.

Opposite: The pleasantly situated campground at Cassells Boykin State Park appears to be well used, but the Parks and Wildlife Department has no staff on the site. The park is administered by the Superintendent of the Martin Dies Jr. State Park, Rt. 4, Box 274, Jasper, TX 75051.

CASSELLS BOYKIN STATE RECREATION AREA

On State Highway 147 about 9 miles east of Zavalla on the west bank of Sam Rayburn Reservoir in Angelina County, 141 miles northeast of Houston. No fee

The U.S. Army Engineers started work in the late 1950s on the dam that created the Sam Rayburn Reservoir. The dam and the lake originally carried the name McGee Bend. Congress changed the name in 1963 to honor Congressman Sam Rayburn of Bonham. Rayburn was Speaker of the House when he died in 1961 at the age of 79.

Sam Rayburn Reservoir was completed in 1965. The Corps of Engineers built this small park north of the Highway 147 bridge on the west shore of the lake. The state took over maintenance when the corps developed budget problems. The site is very pleasantly wooded. A boat ramp is provided. There are no electrical connections, but the park has several campsites and picnic tables and it is well used.

There is no entrance fee here and no one to collect any fees for camping either. The Parks and Wildlife Department has no staff on the grounds. There is no way to make reservations. You just pick the unoccupied site you like. The price is certainly right, but there is no one to complain to if another camper's radio is too loud. Litter could be a problem, but the park has been fairly tidy the times I have seen it.

For more information

It is administered by the superintendent of the Martin Dies Jr. State Park, Rt. 4, Box 274, Jasper, TX 75951. His phone is (409) 384-5231.

Other places to see

Nearby spots of interest are Martin Dies Jr. State Park on Lake B. A. Steinhagen off U.S. 190 and the Corps of Engineers recreation areas in the Angelina National Forest, especially Bouton Lake and Boykin Springs on U.S. 69 south of Zavalla. You will also notice signs throughout the East Texas forest calling attention to forest trails maintained by the Texas Forest Association and the timber companies. They are free and some of them are worth the hike.

MARTIN DIES JR. STATE PARK

Off U.S. 190, 15 miles east of Woodville in Tyler and Jasper counties, 122 miles northeast of Houston. Entrance fee: $2 per car

The Army Corps of Engineers created the lake here in 1951 by building a dam at Town Bluff on the Neches River. It was called Town Bluff Lake originally. It was called Dam B Reservoir for a while until the name was changed to honor the late B. A. Steinhagen of Beaumont. Martin Dies, Jr., represented this area in the state senate. He is the son of the late Congressman Martin Dies. Dies, Sr., represented this district in the U.S. House of Representatives for more than 20 years and headed the House Committee on Un-American Activities during and after World War II.

The western part of the lake is in Tyler County. The eastern part is in Jasper County. The state leased the land for this park from the Corps of Engineers in 1964. There are three units in the park. One is on the west bank and two are on the east bank. The unit on the west bank has boat ramps, picnic sites and restrooms, but no campsites. This is called the Cherokee Unit. It is on both sides of U.S. 190 at the western end of the bridge.

The Walnut Ridge Unit of Martin Dies Jr. State Park is at the eastern end of the bridge on the north side of U.S. 190 on a peninsula; so most of the campsites and picnic sites are close to the water. This unit has 25 screened shelters for $8 a night, 24 campsites with water for $4 a night and 48 sites with water and electricity for $6 a night. There is a boat ramp and a group picnic shelter for rent at $50 a day.

The Henhouse Ridge Unit at the east end of the bridge on the south side of U.S. 190 has more campsites and some screened shelters right on the water. This unit has a small swimming beach, boat ramp, fish-cleaning tables, a trailer camping area and a trailer dump station. There are 44 campsites for $4 a night with water, 24 sites with water and electricity for $6 a night and 32 trailer sites with full hookups for $7 a night. The 21 screened shelters rent for $8 a night. They

Right: The swimming beach in the Henhouse Ridge Unit of Martin Dies Jr. State Park. Most of this lake at the junction of the Neches and Angelina rivers is fairly shallow.

Opposite: Martin Dies Jr. States Park has several screen ed shelters and a number of campsites right on the lake shore where campers can keep their boats handy. Fishing for catfish and crappie is best here in the spring.

have grills, electricity and water, but no plumbing. This is one of the most popular parks in the system. Boat owners like it because they can beach their boats right alongside their shelters or campsites. There is plenty of room for water skiing. Most of the fish caught here are bass and crappie.

The park is in the northern end of the forest area known as the Big Thicket. The trees are cypress, pine, willow, blackgum, oak and dogwood. The park is busiest in the summer. It is prettiest in the spring when the dogwoods are in bloom and in the fall when the hardwoods are changing color. Birdwatchers may see a pileated woodpecker. Hikers probably will see deer and may see a mink, muskrat, fox or beaver. The park has a hiking trail. Visitors may also hike through the Angelina-Neches Scientific Area maintained by the Parks and Wildlife Department north of the park.

I rate this park a little above Huntsville and Livingston. The lake is big enough for all water sports, as the lake in the Huntsville Park is not, and it does not get as rough as Lake Livingston because it is smaller. I think the camping areas are a little more pleasant, too. This is my favorite park in this part of the state.

For more information

Write to Martin Dies Jr. State Park, Rt. 4, Box 274, Jasper, TX 75951 or phone (409) 384-5231 for more information or reservations.

Other places to see

Some other places you might want to visit if you are spending a little time in this park are the Allan Shivers Museum and the Heritage Gardens in Woodville (try the boarding house lunch); the Alabama-Coushatta Indian Reservation on U.S. 190 between Woodville and Livingston ; the Cassells Boykin State Park at Lake Sam Rayburn and the recreation areas the Army Corps of Engineers maintains in the Angelina National Forest, especially Boykin Springs and the nature trail between Boykin Springs and Bouton Lake (accessible from U.S. 69). The Big Thicket National Preserve is several scattered units, some reasonably near here. The Big Thicket National Preserve Visitor Center is about 36 miles south of here off U.S. 69 just south of Village Mills.

SABINE PASS BATTLEGROUND STATE HISTORICAL PARK

On F.M. 3322 off U.S. 87, 1 mile south of the town of Sabine Pass in Jefferson County, 108 miles east of Houston. No fee

There was not a lot of fighting in Texas during the Civil War, but there was some here. Union Gen. William Franklin came to Sabine Pass September 8, 1863, with 20 ships and boats and 5,000 troops. It was supposed to be an invasion.

The 42 Confederates defending the pass had some earthworks and six cannon. The commander was Lt. Dick Dowling of Houston. He was Irish and had been a saloonkeeper in Houston before the war. Several of the other defenders were Irish Houstonians, too.

Franklin sent two gunboats up the channel to knock out Dowling's cannon. Dowling's gunners disabled both gunboats, and the crews surrendered. Gen. Franklin called off the invasion and sailed back to New Orleans. Dowling's men suffered no casualties. They killed 19 Union sailors and captured more than 300 sailors and soldiers. Dowling was a hero.

He did not live long after the war, but Houstonians put up a statue of him in one of their parks.

The Sabine Pass Battleground Park has a Dowling statue, too. A historical marker recalls what happened here in 1863. Nothing is left of the earthworks the Confederates called Fort Griffin. No one is certain exactly where they were because the landscape has changed. Considerable dredging of the Sabine channel was done in the years after the Civil War. Some of the spoil from the channel was dumped here. The U.S. Army had a coastal artillery battery here during World War II.

Some of the bunkers built by the artillerymen are still here, but they were abandoned after World War II and the area was a trash dump when the state bought it in 1971 to create this park.

There are no provisions for camping here and there is no entrance fee. The park is just 56 acres. There are shaded picnic tables, a restroom, a playground, a boat ramp and a fish-cleaning table. Crabbing is pretty good here. There usually are several offshore oil rigs parked next door.

For more information

You can get more information by writing to the Superintendent, Sabine Pass Battleground/Sea Rim State Park, Box 1066, Sabine Pass, TX 77655.

Other places to see

In nearby Beaumont, you can see the replica of the Spindletop boom town of Gladys City on the south side of U.S. 287 and the paddlewheeler *Belle of Beaumont* (on the Neches at the Civic Center). In Port Arthur, see the Pompeiiam Villa, built by Isaac Ellwood when the town was new. Sea Rim State Park is 12 miles farther west on U.S. 87.

Top: A few old bunkers are left at the Sabine Pass Battleground State Historical Park from World War II days.

Left: The state put this memorial on the Sabine Pass Battleground in 1936 because Texas Confederates won a major victory here in 1863. A small force commanded by Lt. Dick Dowling routed a Union invasion fleet. The state marked hundreds of historic sites in 1936 as part of the celebration of the 100th anniversary of the Texas victory at San Jacinto.

SEA RIM STATE PARK

On U.S. 87, 12 miles west of Sabine Pass in Jefferson County, 119 miles east of Houston. Entrance fee: $2 per car

This is the coast resort most accessible to most East Texans. It is a real contrast to the forests and lakes of East Texas. A sea rim marsh is a marsh at the edge of a body of salt water. Part of this park is sea rim marsh. This is the reason for the park's name, but the beach is the biggest attraction.

The state bought the 15,000 acres for this park from the Planet Oil Company and the Horizon Corporation in 1973 and paid a little more than $2 million for it. The park opened in 1977. It has more than five miles of frontage on the Gulf of Mexico and three miles of beach. There are just 20 campsites with water and electricity. They are all in an area close by the bathhouse, right behind the dunes. Camping is allowed on part of the beach, too, and there are some camping platforms on the water trails in the marshland unit of the park.

Highway 87 divides the two units of the park. The beach unit is the narrow area between the highway and the surf. The marshland unit covers a much greater area north of the highway between the highway and the Intracoastal Canal. You cannot see very much of the marshland unit without some kind of boat. A canoe will do, but a boat ramp is provided for motorboats. Maps of the water trails are available and boaters are supposed to file "float plans" when they take off into the marsh. There are some observation platforms on the water trails in addition to the camping platforms. A concessionaire offered tours of the marsh in airboats when the park was new, but he did not do well and he is not here anymore.

Visitors paddling or motoring through the marsh here will see a number of shore and water birds. They may also see some nutria, mink, raccoons, possums, or rabbits, and they almost certainly will see some alligators in the summer. There is also a short nature trail in the beach unit. It is a boardwalk over part of the marsh at the east end of the beach unit. It is called the Gambusia Nature Trail. Hikers, and campers too, will want to have plenty of insect repellant.

This park covers a much greater area than the Galveston Island State Park and has fewer campsites. It never is as crowded as the Galveston Island Park. It is more remote. Some people like it better for this reason. Sea Rim Park is more remote at this writing than it was intended to be. Visitors have to come through

Opposite Top: The section of the Sea Rim State Park fronting on the beach is called the Roy Harrington Beach Unit. Roy Harrington was a member of the legislature and he helped get this land for the Parks and Wildlife Department.

Opposite Bottom: The biggest section of Sea Rim State Park is a marsh with several small lakes and waterways. The sign at the boat ramp in the marsh unit warns visitors to beware of the alligators. An alligator's head is visible in the water just to the left of the sign in this picture.

Port Arthur and Sabine Pass. People could come here from Galveston by way of the Bolivar Ferry and Highway 87 before August, 1983, when Hurricane Alicia washed out Highway 87 between High Island and Sea Rim. The highway is likely to be repaired eventually, but don't head west from here on U.S. 87 without checking with the park rangers.

For more information

You can get more information about Sea Rim State Park or make reservations by writing to the Superintendent, P.O. Box 1066, Sabine Pass, TX 77655 or by calling (409) 971-2559.

Other places to see

Not far from here are the ruins of Confederate Fort Manhassett, 8 miles east of the park on U.S. 87, and the Sabine Pass Battleground State Historical Park, 13 miles east of the park and just south of the town of Sabine Pass.

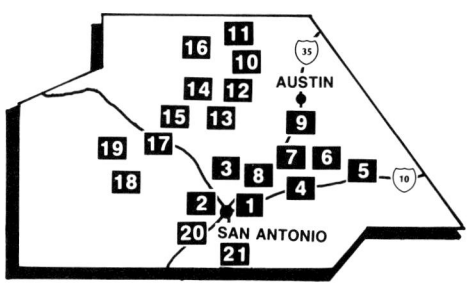

1. San Jose Mission State Historic Site
2. Jose Antonio Navarro State Historic Site
3. Guadalupe River State Park
4. Palmetto State Park
5. Monument Hill/Kreische Brewery State Historic Site
6. Buescher State Park
7. Bastrop State Park
8. Lockhart State Recreation Area
9. McKinney Falls State Park
10. Longhorn Cavern State Park
11. Inks Lake State Park
12. Pedernales Falls State Park
13. Blanco State Recreation Area
14. Lyndon B. Johnson State Historical Park
15. Admiral Nimitz State Historical Park
16. Enchanted Rock State Natural Area
17. Kerrville State Recreation Area
18. Hill Country State Natural Area
19. Lost Maples State Natural Area
20. Garner State Park
21. Landmark Inn State Historic Site

REGION V
PARKS IN SAN ANTONIO AND THE HILL COUNTRY

This section of the state has more state parks than any other and some of the best scenery. Two of the most attractive cities in Texas and one of the most attractive small towns in America are here.

Austin and San Antonio are on everybody's list of desirable places to live. Fredericksburg is everything a small town ought to be.

There are 21 state parks, state recreation areas, state natural areas, state historical parks and state historic sites in this part of the state. Two additional sites are under development.

The parks are arranged here as you would encounter them if you started in San Antonio and followed a rambling counter-clockwise route around the area. I do not think anyone is likely to do this, but it is a way of arranging the parks and showing how far they are from the principal city in the region. The numbers used are just numbers, not ratings. The area has several outstanding parks. My personal favorite is Inks Lake.

Parks Under Development

There is one park under development in this region and one historic structure.

Rancho de las Cabras Historic Site or Archaeological Park is off State Highway 97 outside Floresville in Wilson County. It was an outpost of the Mission San Francisco de la Espada in San Antonio, raising livestock for the missionaries and Indians between 1731 and 1794. There were fortifications and a chapel. Only a few remnants of the foundations remain. The site is 99 acres. The Parks and Wildlife Department bought it in 1976 and 1977 for about $86,000.

Sebastopol House, at West Court and North Erkel in Seguin, was built by Colonel Joshua Young in the 1850s. The building material was concrete. The roof was designed to catch and hold rainwater. The Parks and Wildlife Department bought it from the Seguin Conservation Society in 1977 for $102,557.

SAN JOSE MISSION STATE HISTORIC SITE

On Roosevelt Avenue at Mission Drive, 2 blocks north of Military Drive in south San Antonio. No fee

The oldest mission in San Antonio is the Alamo, established in 1718 in what is now downtown San Antonio. San Jose is the second oldest San Antonio mission. The Mission San Jose y San Miguel de Aguayo was established by the Franciscans in 1720. The mission moved to the present site in 1739. The three other missions here on the south side of San Antonio were established earlier in East Texas and then moved here after San Jose was established. San Francisco de la Espada, San Juan Capistrano and Nuestra Senora de la Purisima Concepcion all moved here in 1731.

All four missions had colonies of Indian converts. They maintained large farms and ranches. The Texas ranching tradition started here at these missions. The first European irrigation system in North America was developed here to serve the mission farms. Fragments of the system of aquaducts or *acequias* built by the missionaries and Indians to carry water from the San Antonio River to their fields still exist and the system is due to be restored.

San Jose and two of the other missions have been restored. Only Concepcion has not. It never fell down. Concepcion is said to be the oldest unrestored stone church in North America. San Jose was abandoned in the middle 1800s. The Indians' and soldiers' quarters around the outer walls fell in. The roof and part of the north wall of the church collapsed in 1868. The dome fell in 1874 and the tower collapsed in 1928. The tower was rebuilt right away and the Franciscans returned to San Jose in 1931. The Catholic Church, the San Antonio Conservation Society, Bexar County and the WPA cooperated in the restoration of the mission buildings and the outer wall. The San Antonio Conservation Society deeded the land to the State Parks Board in 1941 and San Jose was designated a Texas State Historic Site and a National Historic Site.

The old mission still shows up on the list of Texas state parks, but it is also now part of the San Antonio Missions National Park, established in 1983. The people staffing the mission now are National Park Service employees. The National Park Service maintains the grounds around all four missions and probably will restore

The Mission San Jose is the finest surviving example of Spanish colonial architecture in Texas. It is state property but the Mission complex is also part of the San Antonio Missions National Historical Park. There is no fee for admission but donations are accepted and they are tax deductible. Group tours can be arranged by writing to San Antonio Missions National Historical Park, 727 E. Durango, Room A612, San Antonio, TX 78206 or by phoning (512) 922-2731.

the irrigation system, but the National Park Service cannot spend any money on the churches themselves because of what the Constitution says about separation of church and state.

San Jose is an active parish church, holding Mass at 5:30 p.m. Saturdays and at 9 a.m., 10:30 a.m., noon and 5:30 p.m. on Sundays. The church and mission grounds are open to visitors every day from 9 a.m. till 6 p.m. in the summer and 9 a.m. to 5 p.m. the rest of the year. This is generally regarded as the finest Spanish mission in North America and the one to see if you have time to see only one. Espada, San Juan and Concepcion are open, too, and worth seeing.

Other places to see

It would take you days to see everything worth seeing in San Antonio, but you certainly will want to see the Alamo, the old mansions on King William Street, San Fernando Cathedral where the remains of the Alamo defenders are interred, the River Walk, Witte Museum, Tower of the Americas, the Institute of Texan Cultures, the Mercado and the Governor's Palace.

JOSE ANTONIO NAVARRO STATE HISTORIC SITE

228 South Laredo Street in the municipal government complex in downtown San Antonio. Fees: adults $1, children 25¢

Fifty-nine Texans signed the Texas Declaration of Independence at Washington-on-the-Brazos on March 2, 1836. Two of the signers were born in Texas. One of them lived here.

Jose Antonio Navarro was born in San Antonio in 1795. He was a member of the state legislature when Texas and Coahuila were one state in the Mexican Republic. He was a delegate to the Convention of 1836 where the Declaration of Independence was written and he was a member of the committee that drafted the constitution for the Republic of Texas. Navarro also served in the Texas Congress. He went to New Mexico with Mirabeau Lamar's Santa Fe Expedition in 1841 and he was captured there by the Mexicans. Navarro was sentenced to death for his part in that effort to claim New Mexico for Texas. The sentence was commuted and Navarro escaped in 1845. He was back in Texas in time to be a delegate to the Convention of 1845, where he voted for joining the United States.

Navarro was serving in the Texas legislature in 1846 when Navarro County was created and named for him. He was far too old to fight in the Civil War, but he was for secession. All four of his sons served in the Confederate Army.

Navarro operated a store and practiced law when he was not taking part in great political decisions. He lived and conducted his affairs in this complex of small stone buildings at South Laredo and Nueva. The house was built in 1840. Navarro died here in 1891. His daughter inherited the property and later sold it. It changed hands several times before the San Antonio Conservation Society bought it and restored the buildings. The society donated the property to the Parks and Wildlife Department in 1975. The compound is open for tours between 10 a.m. and 4 p.m.

One of the signers of the Texas Declaration of Independence built this home in what is now downtown San Antonio. Jose Navarro lived here until he died in 1871.

Tuesdays through Saturdays. The charge for the tours is $1 for adults, 25 cents for children between 6 and 12. Children under 6 are admitted free. There is a special rate for student groups sponsored by their schools as there is at the other state historic sites where a fee is charged for tours. The student rate is $1 per group. Groups need to make advance reservations.

For more information

The address for more information about the Jose Antonio Navarro State Historic Site is 228 South Laredo Street, San Antonio, TX 78207. The phone number is (512) 226-4801.

Other places to see

The other places you may want to see while you are here are numerous: the Alamo, San Jose and the San Antonio Missions National Park, the River Walk, La Villita, San Fernando Cathedral, Fort Sam Houston and Brackenridge Park and Zoo. The home of the only other native Texan to sign the Declaration of Independence is on the grounds of the Witte Museum in Brackenridge Park. The other native was Jose Francisco Ruiz. He was born in San Antonio, too.

GUADALUPE RIVER STATE PARK

On State Highway 46, 8 miles west of the U.S. 281 intersection, in Kendall and Comal counties, 30 miles north of San Antonio. Entrance fee: $2 per car

The Guadalupe River is the river most Texans like most. It is a special favorite of rafting and canoeing enthusiasts. This park offers those folks a good place to get their rafts and canoes in and out of the water.

The Parks and Wildlife Department bought the 1,900 acres here in 1975 and 1976. The first section of the park opened in June, 1983. This section is 1,239 acres on the south side of the river. The 661-acre section on the north side of the river is undeveloped and not open.

The section of the park that is open has one and one-half miles of river frontage. This is the Guadalupe at its best — limestone cliffs, bald cypress trees and clear water. There are four rapids within the park.

The picnic area is the prettiest part of this park. There are 50 tables and grills scattered along the bank of the river, not too close together. The trees besides the cypress are pecan, sycamore, hackberry, persimmon, willow and basswood. There is one stand of virgin Ashe juniper, so birdwatchers are able to see the golden-cheeked warbler here. The warbler is said to be the only bird that nests only in Texas. The golden-cheeked warbler makes its nests of nothing but Ashe juniper. The birds winter in Central America. They come to the Hill County in March, start their families here and return to Central America in late summer. This park is full of them in the spring and early summer.

Hikers may see deer, coyotes, grey foxes, possums or raccoons in the woods here or on the adjacent Texas Nature Conservancy property. The Nature Conservancy has made a preserve of the old Doppenschmidt-Honey Creek Ranch. It

Left: The Guadalupe River State Park opened in the summer of 1983. The Guadalupe is one of the most picturesque rivers in Texas

Opposite: The Guadalupe River is one of the canoeists' favorite Texas streams.

is open only to guided tours; the park office has information about the tours.

Most of the early settlers in this part of Texas were German farmers. They came in the 1840s and 1850s and had better luck getting along with the Comanches than some other settlers did. Part of this park was once the Phillip Bauer farm. Bauer came from Prussia in 1854.

The 48 campsites in this park have water, electricity, tables and grills and rent for $6 a night. The 37 tent campsites on the north side of the river are $4 a night. There are no group shelters here.

For more information

The address for reservations or more information about the Guadalupe River State Park is P.O. Box 28, Bergheim, TX 78004. The phone number is (512) 438-2656.

Other places to see

Other places near by are San Antonio, 37 miles south; Blanco State Recreation Area, 30 miles north on U.S. 281; Johnson City, 40 miles north on U.S. 281, where the National Park Service maintains President Lyndon Johnson's boyhood home and his grandfather's log cabin; San Marcos, 53 miles northeast (Aquarena Springs); and New Braunfels, 29 miles east on State 46 (Comal River and several historic buildings).

The Natural Bridge Cavern, Century Caverns and Cascade Caverns are all within about 30 miles of Guadalupe River State Park.

PALMETTO STATE PARK

Off U.S. 183, halfway between Luling and Gonzales in Gonzales County, 60 miles east of San Antonio.
Entrance fee: $2 per car

This park was established in the early days of the CCC park development program because the terrain here is so unusual. The National Park Service listed it at the time as the only palmetto swamp of its kind in the Southwest. The San Marcos River runs through here. The swamp conditions are caused partly by overflow from the occasional floods on the river and partly by warm sulphur springs. The small oxbow lake in the park is actually a former channel of the San Marcos.

The 263 acres making up this park were deeded to the state in 1933 by the city of Gonzales, the Texas and New Orleans Railroad and several individual property owners. Most of the park is swampy, but there are some bluffs along the river. Fishing and swimming are good in the lake. There are three trails for hikers and a lot of birds to watch. Two hundred and forty species have been observed here. The park has a playground and three picnic grounds. There are 19 campsites with water and electricity for $6 a night and 18 primitive campsites reasonably close to water taps for $4 a night. The restrooms in the camping areas have showers.

Swamps attract insects; so you will want to bring plenty of repellant. The park and campgrounds are open the year round. Fall is usually the most pleasant time of year here.

The Palmetto State Park occupies part of an area known as the Ottine Swamp. The swamp took its name from the town of Ottine. The town was named by early settler Adolph Otto. Mrs. Otto's name was Christine. The founder combined the first syllable of his last name with the last syllable of his wife's first name to make a name for his town.

Thousands of polio victims were treated here before the vaccines were developed. The Texas Warm Springs Foundation for Crippled Children was established adjacent to the park in 1937 to provide treatments similar to those President Roosevelt was then receiving at Warm Springs, Georgia. The Texas Rehabilitation Center and Elks Hospital at the same site now provide rehabilitation treatment for victims of other diseases and accidents.

For more information

You can make reservations or get more information about Palmetto State Park by writing the Superintendent at Rt. 2, Box 66D, Gonzales, TX 78629. The phone number is (512) 672-3266.

Other places to see

Gonzales, just 14 miles to the southeast, is where the Texas Revolution really started in October, 1836. The town has two museums and several historic buildings, including an 1895 courthouse. San Marcos and Aquarena Springs are just 34 miles to the northwest. The Lockhart State Recreation Area and golf course are about 25 miles north of Palmetto State Park. Lockhart also has a good campground.

Top: This dining hall in Palmetto State Park can accommodate up to 100 people. There is no fee for using it, but reservations are necessary. The National Park Service has called this one of the outstanding park buildings in the country. It was built of native stone by the CCC in 1934.

Right: Parts of Palmetto State Park resemble a tropical forest. Wild orchids and other exotic plants grow here.

MONUMENT HILL/KREISCHE BREWERY STATE HISTORIC SITE

Off U.S. 77 just south of LaGrange in Fayette County, 116 miles northeast of San Antonio.
Entrance fee: adults $1, children 25¢

Monument Hill has been a state park for a long time. The Parks and Wildlife Department bought the Kreische Brewery in 1977. The two properties are next to each other on a bluff on the south bank of the Colorado, overlooking the river valley and the city of LaGrange. The view from here is probably the most inspiring in Fayette County. This is the reason the monument that gives the hill its name is located here. The monument is a tribute to some of the early heroes of Texas.

The remains of 52 men killed in encounters with the Mexicans in 1842 and 1843 are buried here.

The 1842 encounter occurred outside San Antonio in September. Nicholas Mosby Dawson and 53 men from here were on their way to help turn back a new Mexican invasion. They were surprised by a superior Mexican cavalry force. Dawson and 34 of his men were killed. Other Texans routed the invaders and President Sam Houston ordered a retaliatory sally into Mexico. Gen. Alexander Somervell and 700 volunteers swept through Guerrero and Laredo in December, 1842. Somervell thought that was enough. He and most of the Texans withdrew. Col. William Fisher and 308 Texans decided to stay south of the border a little longer. They met a lot of resistance when they tried to take the border town of Mier. The Texans surrendered to the defenders. Some of the Texans tried to escape as they were being marched to Mexico City. They were caught and President Santa Anna ordered every tenth one of them to be executed.

The prisoners were forced to gamble for their lives by drawing beans out of a pot. Those drawing white beans were allowed to live. Those drawing black beans were shot at Salado in March, 1843. The first man to draw a black bean was Capt. William Mosby Eastland of Fayette County. The remains of all 17 of the executed Texans were brought to LaGrange after they were found by American troops during the Mexican War in 1846. The remains of Capt. Nicholas Dawson and his men were brought here from Bexar County about the same time. They were all interred in a vault on this hill on September 18, 1848, at a solemn ceremony attended by Senator Sam Houston and many other Texas patriots. The Daughters of the Republic of Texas raised the money in 1907 to buy the ground around the tomb

A German immigrant named Henry Kreische bought the property adjacent to Monument Hill in 1849. The brewery he built is in ruins. The Kreische house is still standing. It will be open for tours when the Parks and Wildlife Department finishes repairing it in 1985. The grounds are open 365 days a year.

for the state. The state put up the monument in 1936 during the Centennial celebration.

There was nothing much here for a long time except the vault and the monument and a few picnic tables. There is some additional room and some interesting ruins now that the state has bought the old brewery next door. The Kreische home and brewery occupied 36 acres on the bluff. This section of the park is open to tours, but the house and the ruins of the brewery are still being restored. They should be open in 1985.

There is no campground here and no room for one; so this park is open only during the daytime and the fee is less than in the regular state parks. It is $1 for adults and 25 cents for children. The fee is waived for holders of senior citizens' passports.

For more information

You can get more information about the Monument Hill/Kreische Brewery State Historic Site from the Superintendent, Rt. 1, Box 699, LaGrange, TX 78945. The phone number is (409) 968-5658.

Other places to see

Several picturesque small towns besides LaGrange are within a short distance of this park, notably Round Top (16 miles north), Fayetteville (16 miles east), New Ulm (30 miles east) and Columbus (26 miles southeast).

Four state parks are within 70 miles of here. They are Buescher off State Highway 71 outside of Smithville; Bastrop off State Highway 71 outside of Bastrop; Lockhart off U.S. 183 south of Lockhart; and Palmetto off U.S. 183 between Luling and Gonzales. All four have good campgrounds.

BUESCHER STATE PARK

Off State Highway 71 on F.M. 153, 2 miles northwest of Smithville in Bastrop County, 108 miles northeast of San Antonio. Entrance fee: $2 per car

The western edge of the main Texas pine forest is 80 miles east of here, but there is an island of loblolly pines here in Bastrop County. The lumber for the original buildings in Austin came from here. These are the Lost Pines of Texas. They are the main reason for the Buescher and Bastrop parks.

The trees in this park are not all pines. There are also some old oak trees draped with Spanish moss. The area was part of the Stephen F. Austin colony in colonial days. This park is on land granted to one of Austin's colonists.

The property for this park was donated by the city of Smithville and Mrs. Elizabeth Buescher and her family in the 1930s. The original improvements were made by the CCC. The park was 1,730 acres until 1969 when the Parks and Wildlife Department transferred 717 acres to M. D. Anderson Hospital to be used for medical and ecological research. That part of the park is known now as the U.T. Environmental Science Park.

Buescher Park is arranged around a lake that is big enough for swimming and fishing, but too small for serious boating or skiing. There are 65 picnic sites on the east side of the lake and campgrounds on the east and west sides. This park has 26 tent campsites with water for $4 a night and 40 sites with water, electricity, table and grill for $6 a night. One group picnic shelter is available at $16 a day. A recreation hall with kitchen rents for $55 a day. The park conducts drawings every January 11 for the shelter and recreation hall because sometimes several groups want one or the other of these the same day. Both can be reserved in the regular way for dates not claimed through the drawings.

There are four screened shelters on the east bank of the lake for rent at $8 a night. Restrooms in the shelter area and in the camping areas have showers. There are no hiking trails in his park, but there is a 14-mile scenic drive between Buescher and Bastrop state parks.

For more information

You can make reservations or get more information about Buescher State Park by writing to the Superintendent, P.O. Box 75, Smithville, TX 78957 or by calling (512) 237-2241.

Other places to see

Other places are the old Wendish church at Serbin on F.M. 2239, 20 miles northeast; Bastrop State Park and the town of Bastrop, 12 miles northwest on State Highway 71; Austin, 42 miles northwest on State Highway 71; and Lockhart State Recreation Area, 49 miles southwest on U.S. 183 south of Lockhart.

A park road connects Buescher State Park with Bastrop State Park. It is scenic. It is also narrow and crooked and it should be negotiated with caution.

BASTROP STATE PARK

Off State Highway 71 just east of Bastrop in Bastrop County, 96 miles northeast of San Antonio. Entrance fee: $2 per car

Bastrop State Park was created in the 1930s when the CCC was building parks to create jobs for unemployed young men. Few such programs have produced such lasting benefits. The city of Bastrop, the Vaughn Lumber Company and several individuals gave the state the original 2,100 acres here. The Parks and Wildlife Department bought another 1,400 acres in 1979; so this is one of our larger parks and it has about everything a park can have except frontage on a big lake or river.

The lake here is a very small one. The Colorado River is a couple of miles away. But Bastrop Park has a pine and oak forest, a golf course, a swimming pool, campgrounds and cabins and provisions for groups of up to 100 people.

The pines here are some of the Lost Pines of Texas, about 80 miles west of the main pine forest in East Texas. The pines supposedly got started here during the Pleistocene Period because the climate was wetter then and because the soil was and is porous and acidic due to deposits laid down by the Colorado when it was a much bigger river.

This area was part of Stephen F. Austin's colony before the Texas Revolution. The town of Bastrop was established in 1829 at the point where the old Camino Real crossed the Colorado. State Highway 21 along the west boundary of the park follows the route of the Camino Real. Some of the great personalities of the early days passed this way. Davy Crockett came by here on his way to the Alamo.

Birds and birdwatchers are attracted to the forest here. The park office has checklists of the birds you can expect to find in Bastrop and Buescher parks. There is a hiking trail and a scenic drive connecting with Buescher Park to the east.

The nine-hole golf course in Bastrop Park is operated by the Lost Pines Golf Association. The greens fee is $4 for weekdays and $5 on weekends and holidays. Golf carts are available for rent. The golf course is open year-round.

The swimming pool is open only during the summer. The admission fee is $1 for adults and 50 cents for children.

There are 13 cabins of different sizes on the little lake here. Some hold only two or three people and some will accommodate five or six. There is one over-size cabin, accommodating eight people. This one rents for $40 a night. The other cabins are $18 for the first one or two people, $4 for each additional adult and $1 for each additional child. The 13 cabins are numbered 1 through 12 and the last one has the number 14 so nobody has to spend the night in a cabin with the number 13. The cabins have kitchens and baths. Linens and bedding are furnished. Dishes and utensils are not.

There are three campgrounds here. Twenty-eight of the campsites have water, table and grill and rent for $4 a night. The 27 sites with water, electricity, table and grill rent for $6 a night. The 25 sites with water, electricity, sewer connections, table and grill rent for $7 a night. There also are provisions for primitive camping along the hiking trail.

Bastrop has a refectory, or dining hall, for large groups. The hall has a large meeting and dining room, patio, kitchen and restrooms. It can accommodate up to 90 people. It rents for day use only for $40.

The group lodge here can accommodate up to 90 people overnight. It has a large kitchen with stove, refrigerator, tables and chairs, and four dorms with cots and bunk beds. The rent is $100 a night. No bedding, linens, dishes or utensils are furnished.

The dining hall and group lodge can be reserved and rented for any dates that have not been claimed through the January 11 drawing.

For more information

You can make reservations or get more information by writing to the Superintendent, Bastrop State Park, Box 518, Bastrop, TX 78602 or by calling (512) 321-2101.

Other places to see

Some places you may want to see in this area are Buescher State Park off State Highway 71 at Smithville; Lake Somerville State Recreation Area about 50 miles northeast; Monument Hill/Kreische Brewery State Historic Site, 31 miles southeast at LaGrange; Palmetto State Park, 55 miles south; Lockhart State Recreation Area, 37 miles southwest; and McKinney Falls State Park, 35 miles west.

The city of Bastrop has a number of historic homes, buildings and churches. Austin is just 30 miles away.

The original buildings in Bastrop State Park were built of native stone and hand hewn pine by the men of the Civilian Conservation Corps. This is the recreation hall. There is a swimming pool nearby.

LOCKHART STATE RECREATION AREA

3 miles south of Lockhart off F.M. 20, west of U.S. 183 in Caldwell County, 72 miles northeast of San Antonio. Entrance fee: $2 per car

The golf course is the principal attraction in this park. It was rented to the Lockhart Country Club for about 10 years until 1948. It has been operating as a park since then. People in the area still play here. Some campers drag their golf carts when they come here, the same way other campers drag their boats to other parks.

The city of Lockhart and Caldwell County acquired the 257 acres here from various individuals and transferred the property to the State Parks Board in 1933. The National Park Service drew up the plans and the CCC started work here in 1936. The CCC built the golf course, the recreation hall and the original swimming pool. A new swimming pool was built in 1973. The golf course has been altered some. It is a nine-hole course. It is the only course operated by the Parks and Wildlife Department. The courses at Inks Lake, Bastrop and Stephen F. Austin are operated by local golf associations.

The greens fee is $3 for weekdays and $4 on weekends and holidays; there is a $1 trail fee for golf carts. Annual rates and annual family rates are available. The swimming pool fees are the same in all the parks: $1 for adults and 50 cents for children.

This park has four primitive campsites for $4 a night. There are 10 sites with water, electricity, table and grill for $6 a night and 10 trailer sites with water, electricity, sewer connections, table and grill for $7 a night.

The recreation hall here is available for rent at $40 a day for day use only. The hall includes a patio, picnic area, playground and restrooms. The hall has a kit-

The nine-hole golf course in the Lockhart State Recreation Area is operated by the Parks and Wildlife Department. Concessionaires operate the other courses in the system. It has been changed some since, but the CCC built the golf course here in the 1930s.

chen, but no stove or refrigerator. There is an additional charge of $15 a day for use of the kitchen. This hall can be rented overnight for $70, or $85 with the kitchen.

The only water here besides the swimming pool is a little creek called Clear Fork or Plum Creek. They say there are bass and catfish in it and fishing is allowed, but you won't need your boat. It is a very modest little creek in normal times. A picnic area near the pool has 10 tables. The golf course occupies most of the property; so there is no hiking trail. There are some deer and smaller animals and lots of birds.

One of the big Indian battles of the 1840s was fought near here. A band of Comanches rode down the Guadalupe in the summer of 1840 to get revenge for the losses they had suffered in the Council House fight in San Antonio the previous March. The Indians plundered and burned the town of Linnville in Calhoun County and started back to the plains. Texas Rangers and a volunteer army caught up with the raiders here near Lockhart. The Comanches lost the ensuing battle and they did not come this far south again.

For more information

You can write to the Superintendent, Lockhart State Recreation Area, Rt. 1, Box 69, Lockhart, TX 78644 or call (512) 398-3479 if you want to make reservations or get information about this park.

Other places to see

Some other places to see while you are in this area are Palmetto State Park, 23 miles south on U.S. 183; San Marcos and Aquarena Springs, 19 miles west on State Highway 142; Austin, 30 miles north of U.S. 183; Bastrop State Park, 37 miles northeast off State Highway 71; and Buescher State Park, 46 miles northeast off State Highway 71.

MCKINNEY FALLS STATE PARK

Off Scenic Loop Road, west of U.S. 183, 7 miles south of Austin in Travis County about 80 miles northeast of San Antonio.
Entrance fee: $2 per car

This park is so handy to Austin that some people would live here if they could. All the state park campgrounds have a rule against anyone staying more than 14 consecutive days. Campers can leave for a weekend and then come back for another 14 days in most of the parks. There is a special rule for this park. Campers have to be gone for 14 days before they can come back for another 14 days. Some campers have changed cars and even changed their names to try to get around this rule. Some people working in Austin are that anxious to live in tents or trailers in McKinney Falls Park. The proximity to Austin is not the only reason. The rent is cheap and it is a very nice park.

This property was once the home of one of the important citizens of Texas. Thomas F. McKinney was born in Kentucky and was a trader in Missouri before he came to Texas in 1824 as one of Stephen F. Austin's colonists. He was a partner in a lumber business with Michel B. Menard and a partner with Samuel May Williams in a cotton factoring and banking business before 1836. McKinney and Williams bought shares in Menard's Galveston City Company. McKinney and Williams built the first wharf in Galveston. They helped finance the Texas Revolution although it is not clear whether they knew they would not be repaid for the supplies and munitions they bought. Williams stayed in Galveston until he died. Thomas McKinney moved to Travis County in 1853 and started a grist mill and horse farm on this property. He prospered until the Civil War. The war ruined him and he was a poor man when he died in 1873.

The McKinney property was donated to the state in 1970 by Mr. and Mrs. J. E. Smith and Annie M. Smith. It is 632 acres surrounding the junction of Williamson Creek and Onion Creek. The park has almost two miles of creek frontage. Onion Creek alternates between quiet pools and rapids. The two waterfalls within the park are known as Upper Falls and McKinney Falls. This is limestone and juniper country, but there are bald cypress, oaks, elms, sycamores and hackberry trees along the creeks.

The park has a variety of songbirds, some deer and some wild turkeys. There are 113 picnic sites plus playgrounds in the picnic and camping areas. A hike-

One of the two small waterfalls on Onion Creek in McKinney Falls State Park.

and-bike trail loops around the campgrounds and along the bank of Onion Creek. A hiking trail runs from the visitor center along the bank of Onion Creek to an old Indian rock shelter under a limestone ledge.

There are 14 tent campsites here with water, table and grill for $4 a night. Seventy sites have water, electricity, table and grill for $6. The park has a group camping area and a group dining hall. They are in demand and drawings are held January 11 to determine which applicants get what dates. The dining hall accommodates 70 people and rents for $50 a day. It has a kitchen, refrigerator and freezer. The dining hall and the six screened shelters in the group camp can be rented together for $100.

For more information

To make reservations or get more information about McKinney Falls State Park, you can call (512) 243-1643 or write to the Superintendent, Rt. 2, Box 701B, Austin, TX 78744.

Other places to see

The northwestern boundary of this park is a municipal golf course. The State Capitol is just 13 miles away. You may also want to visit some of the other Austin landmarks while you are here like the Lyndon B. Johnson Library on the U.T. campus, the Bremond block, the Hirschfield houses and the O'Henry house downtown, and the Ney Museum at 304 East 44th.

Pedernales Falls State Park is just 40 miles west of here. Bastrop and Buescher state parks are less than 40 miles to the east. Lockhart State Recreation Area is 25 miles to the south. All four of these parks have good campgrounds.

LONGHORN CAVERN STATE PARK

On Park Road 4, west of U.S. 281, 11 miles southwest of Burnet in Burnet County, 88 miles north of San Antonio. Fees: adults $4, children $3.

The Texas State Parks Board was concerned in the 1930s with administering and managing parks donated to the state by cities, counties and individuals. The Parks Board had no money to spend buying parks, but the board bought two parks, anyway. Palo Duro Canyon and Longhorn Cavern were bought on the installment plan.

The board bought the biggest part of the Longhorn Cavern land in 1932 from Dr. and Mrs. J. L. Williamson, promising to pay $6,567 for the 456 acres in seven years with interest at 7 percent. Part of the purchase price actually was paid out of special funds. The rest was paid out of income from the cave. The board contracted with a concessionaire to operate the park and conduct tours of the cavern. The concessionaire paid the board 20 percent of the revenue. Half of that went to the Williamsons until the debt was paid off. Several smaller tracts have been added to the original 456 acres. The park is still operated by a concessionaire. The Parks and Wildlife Department is still collecting a percentage of the take from admission fees and sales of snacks and souvenirs. Longhorn Cavern State Park has more than paid for itself.

The present admission fees are $4 for adults and $3 for children between 4 and 12. Children under 4 get in free. There is no fee for the use of the part of this park that is above ground. This part includes 10 picnic tables, a hiking trail and a lookout tower. One of the best things about this park is the scenery along Park Road 4 between U.S. 281 and here and between here and Inks Lake State Park.

Longhorn Cavern is the biggest cave in Texas and one of the biggest in the country. It had been called Hoover's Valley Cave and Sherrard's Cave before the Parks Board bought it and gave it the present name. It had been used for various purposes before 1932 and not all the purposes were legal. The outlaw Sam Bass supposedly hid out here at least once in the 1870s. Some people say there was a speak-easy in the cave during the Roaring Twenties. There definitely was a gunpowder factory here during the Civil War. The factory was not underground because of the threat of Union attack but because the stuff they were making the gunpowder from was in the cave. Generations of bats had generated mountains of dung, rich in nitrates. The state put some convicts to work clearing the

Visitors entering Longhorn Cavern. The tours are conducted every day during the summer, but the cavern is closed on Mondays and Tuesdays between October and February.

bat dung and other debris out of here in 1932. The CCC came in 1934 and put in the lighting and built a stone administration building. The park was dedicated on Thanksgiving Day, 1932, by former governor Pat Neff. Bats do not live here in any great numbers any more because many of the openings they used in their comings and goings have been closed off.

The temperature in the cave is a constant 64 degrees year-round; so you'll be more comfortable with a sweater than without. The cave is open every day during the summer. It is closed Mondays and Tuesdays during the winter (October through February).

For more information

If you want more information about Longhorn Cavern State Park, you can write to Ronnie White, Rt. 2, Box 23, Burnet, TX 78611 or call (512) 756-4680.

Other places to see

You should visit Inks Lake State Park while you are here. It's just 6 miles on down Park Road 4. You may also want to see Fort Croghan in Burnet; Buchanan Dam, just west of the park on State Highway 29; and the granite quarry at Marble Falls. The Pedernales Falls State Park is just 45 miles to the south on F.M. 2766 east of U.S. 281.

INKS LAKE STATE PARK

On Park Road 4 about 10 miles west of Burnet in Burnet County, 98 miles north of San Antonio. Entrance fee: $2 per car

Park Road 4 links up with State Highway 29 west of Burnet and with U.S. 281 south of Burnet. Turn left onto Park Road 4, 5 miles south of Burnet if you are approaching from the south. Highway 29 is the best way to get to Inks Lake State Park if you are in Burnet or coming in from the north, east or west.

This is the second most popular camping park in the system. Only Garner draws bigger crowds. This does not mean that Inks Lake is almost as crowded as Garner. It has more land and lots more water; so people do not have to get as close to each other. Inks Lake seems to get more young families and fewer young singles.

Some families come here year after year to spend a week or two by the lake. Many bring their boats. The lake is big enough for skiing and almost any kind of boat. The park has a boat ramp, fishing piers and fish-cleaning tables. A park store sells camping supplies and rents boats. Black bass attract fishermen here. Divers enjoy the lake, too.

The Lower Colorado River Authority was created by the legislature in 1934 to build dams to control flooding and generate electricity. The first lake the Authority built was Buchanan, just north of here. Inks was the Authority's second lake. It was named for Roy Inks of Llano. He was a director of the Lower Colorado River Authority. He died shortly before this lake was completed in 1938.

The act creating the River Authority directed the Authority to provide land for a state park below Buchanan Dam. This park is on the 1,200 acres the River Authority provided. The original improvements were built by the CCC.

This area is part of the mineral region sometimes called the Llano Uplift. The stone here is pink gneiss and granite. Lichens growing on the boulders scattered around the park give them a variety of colors. Campers and hikers may occasionally get a glimpse of a deer or a wild turkey.

The park has a nine-hole golf course, playgrounds and campsites ranging from primitive to screened. There is a primitive camping area for backpackers on the hiking trail at the south end of the park.

The main campgrounds have 143 tent campsites with water for $4 a night and 54 sites with water and electricity for $6 a night. All these campsites have tables

Left: Inks Lake State Park is popular with young families and the lighted fishing pier is popular with the youngsters. A park store sells fishing supplies and rents small boats. There is a federal fish hatchery, open to visitors, at the dam.

Opposite: The rocks along what was the bank of the Colorado River before the dam was built give Inks Lake a special character.

and grills. This park also has 22 screened shelters for rent at $8 a night. There are 15 picnic sites and two group picnic areas. An amphitheater on the lake shore is the site of slide shows and movies on summer evenings.

The golf course in this park is operated by the Highland Lakes Golf Club, Inc. The greens fee is $5 for weekdays and $6 for weekends and holidays. Clubs, pull carts and electric carts are available for rent.

There are no group camps here, but Inks Lake State Park has just about everything else except private bathrooms.

For more information

You need reservations and you can make them or get more information by calling (512) 793-2223 or by writing to the Superintendent, Box 117, Buchanan Dam, TX 78609.

Other places to see

Other places you may want to see in this area are Old Fort Croghan in Burnet, 10 miles east; Fort Hood, 60 miles northeast at Killeen (still an active base but open to the public; has a museum); and Enchanted Rock State Natural Area, 49 miles southwest on F.M. 965.

PEDERNALES FALLS STATE PARK

Off Ranch Road 2766, 14 miles east of Johnson City in Blanco County, 80 miles north of San Antonio. Entrance fee: $2 per car

The rest of the world learned while Lyndon Johnson was president that the name of the river here is not pronounced the way it is spelled. The president called it the "PERD-n-alice." Most people in this area pronounce it approximately that way, too. There once was a little German settlement on the river with the same name. *Pedernales* means flint rocks in Spanish. A great many flint arrow points have been found along the river.

This river flows through the LBJ Ranch. Lyndon Johnson felt very possessive about the Pedernales, but it flows through and around a lot of other property, too. The Pedernales rises in Kimble County and joins the Colorado in western Travis County. It is 106 miles long. This park has nine miles of frontage on the river. The C. A. Wheatleys of San Antonio bought this property in 1937. They called it the Circle Bar Ranch and they raised cattle here for 30 years. The Wheatleys wanted their ranch to be a park and they tried twice to give it to the state. They wanted it to be kept up and they were not impressed with the way the state was maintaining parks at the time. That was before admission fees were established and the Parks Board did not have a lot of money. Some of the parks were run down.

The Wheatleys offered to give the ranch to the state in 1962 if the Parks Board would promise to spend half a million dollars on it. The board could not make that commitment and the offer was declined. The Wheatleys then said they would donate the property if the board would promise to spend a quarter of a million dollars on it. The board agreed to that, but the legislature never got around to appropriating the money. The deal fell through. The legislature voted in 1963 to combine the Parks Board and the Game and Fish Commission into a new Parks and Wildlife Department. The park admission fees were established in 1968. Revenue bonds were sold and the new department had some money to spend by 1969. The Wheatleys had decided they wanted to be paid for their land by that time. The Parks and Wildlife Department bought the ranch for $930,465 and the park opened in 1970.

The river and the hiking trails are the big attractions here. There are quiet pools and some rapids and falls on the Pedernales within the park. Visitors swim and

The falls that give Pedernales Falls State Park its name are not very impressive when the weather is as dry as it was in the summer of 1984 when this picture was made. But this area is subject to flash floods when there is a lot of rain.

wade and ride rafts. There is not a lot of fishing. This river and all the streams in the Hill Country are subject to flash flooding. Signs warn visitors about the possibility of flooding and sirens alert visitors when a flood is coming down the river. There is plenty of high ground to move to when this happens. Most of the park is hilly and the campgrounds are high.

This park has 69 campsites with water, electricity, table and grill for $6 a night. There is a primitive campground on the Wolf Mountain hiking trail. This trail is seven miles long. The primitive campground has no conveniences beyond chemical toilets. I have heard complaints about overcrowding in the primitive campground here, but the park superintendent says they are unfounded. There are 21 primitive campsites for $4 a night. No camping is allowed outside the designated areas.

For more information

You can make reservations or get more information about this park by calling (512) 868-7304 or by writing to the Superintendent at Rt. 1, Box 31A, Johnson City, TX 78636.

Other places to see

Other sights in this area are Johnson City, 14 miles west; the home where Lyndon Johnson lived as a boy and the log cabin his grandfather lived in are maintained by the National Park Service and are open to visitors. Stonewall, 30 miles west (where the LBJ Ranch is maintained by the National Park Service and free bus tours begin from the Lyndon B. Johnson State Park on Ranch Road 1 opposite the ranch); and Blanco State Recreation Area in Blanco, 28 miles southwest on U.S. 281.

BLANCO STATE RECREATION AREA

In Blanco on U.S. 281 in Blanco County, 63 miles north of San Antonio.
Entrance fee: $2 per car

This park, the town and county take their names from the Blanco River. The river was named by one of the early Spanish explorers. *Blanco* is Spanish for white. The water is not white, but the limestone river bed is.

This small park is one of our older ones. The 105 acres here were deeded to the Parks Board between 1936 and 1940 by 17 families and individuals. The CCC built the original improvements. The Blanco River is fed by springs in the limestone hills. It does not carry a large volume of water in normal times. The CCC built two small dams in the park so there would be plenty of water for swimming and fishing. Only small boats are allowed. A concessionaire has pedal boats for rent. The original dams are still in place and the clubhouse the CCC built is in good condition, too.

The Parks and Wildlife Department gave this park an overhaul in 1982-83 and added some camping and picnic sites. The park is on both sides of the river and about a mile long. There are 37 picnic sites on the river banks plus a group picnic area. The old CCC clubhouse overlooks the river and is available for parties and meetings. It has its own kitchen and restrooms. It rents for $8 a day for groups up to 25 or $16 a day for groups of 26 to 150. Use of the kitchen is an additional $15.

This park has 10 trailer campsites with water, electricity, sewer connections, table and grill for $7 a night. There are 21 campsites with water, electricity, table and grill for $6 a night and five primitive camping sites at $4 a night. There are six screened shelters overlooking the river for rent at $8 a night.

The restrooms in the camping area have showers. The water is heated by the sun in the park system's first solar heating unit. There are three playgrounds. Any supplies you need can be bought in Blanco. It is close enough to walk to, but walkers probably will prefer to hike in the park. There are many deer in the area, but they seldom venture into the park. Many species of birds live here or migrate through here. This is a pleasant spot to spend a few hours and a convenient place to spend a few days. It seems to attract a lot of young families.

For more information

The address for reservations or more information is Superintendent, Blanco State Recreation Area, Box 493, Blanco, TX 78606. The phone number is (512) 833-4333.

Other places to see

The town of Blanco was the county seat from the time Blanco County was organized in 1858 until the government moved to Johnson City in 1891. The old courthouse is still standing in downtown Blanco. Not much goes on there now.

The Admiral Nimitz State Historic Site at Fredericksburg, the LBJ Ranch, Lyndon B. Johnson State Historical Park, Johnson City and the Johnson homes, Longhorn Cavern, Pedernales Falls State Park, Guadalupe River State Park and the cities of Austin and San Antonio are all within an hour's drive of the Blanco State Recreation Area.

The CCC built the original buildings here and put the dams across the Blanco River to create the lakes in the 1930s. The stone clubhouse overlooking the lake can be rented by the day.

LYNDON B. JOHNSON STATE HISTORICAL PARK

U.S. 290 at Stonewall in Gillespie County, 79 miles northwest of San Antonio. No entrance fee

Lyndon Johnson was concerned that speculators would buy up the land across the road from his ranch and build souvenir stands and beer halls after he became president. George Brown of Houston and some of the president's other rich friends bought the land and gave it to the Parks and Wildlife Department. This made Johnson happy and Texans got a really nice park out of it. The park was just 269 acres when it was dedicated in 1970 at ceremonies attended by the Johnson family. It is 718 acres now. The LBJ Ranch fronts on Ranch Road 1. The highway department gave the road this designation when Johnson became president. This park occupies most of the land between Ranch Road 1 and U.S. 290 opposite the ranch.

The National Park Service conducts free bus tours of the LBJ Ranch. They begin from the visitor center in the Lyndon B. Johnson State Historical Park. The Johnsons gave the LBJ Ranch to the federal government. Mrs. Johnson retains the right to use the house and she visits the state park here several times a year. She gives prizes every year to the highway department employees with the best record for beautifying the roadsides. Those presentations usually take place in the little amphitheater outside the visitor center here.

Camping is prohibited in this park, but Blanco State Park and Pedernales Falls State Park are within 30 miles and they both have good campgrounds. The Lady Bird Johnson Municipal Park south of Fredericksburg also has campgrounds and is only about 17 miles from here. There are individual picnic sites here and a group dining hall and a group picnic shelter. There is no fee for the individual sites. The group shelter rents for $16 a day and it can accommodate up to 200 people. The dining hall has a kitchen. It can accommodate up to 80 people and it rents for $50 a day.

The park has two tennis courts, a baseball diamond and a large swimming pool. The fee for the pool is $1 for adults and 50 cents for children. The pool can be rented for private parties in the evenings for $35.

A statue of President Johnson stands in a little grove in the park. His voice is reproduced in some of the audio-visual programs in the visitor center. Reminders of him are everywhere, but this park also has some features that have little to do with the Johnsons.

Three pioneer log cabins are preserved in the park. One of them stands in a patch of wildflowers (in season) between the pool and the main parking lot. One of them is incorporated into the visitor center. The third one is part of the Sauer-Beckman farmstead. The farmstead is the most unusual feature of this park.

The John Sauers built the first building in this complex, with logs, in the 1860s. They added a stone cottage later. The Emil Beckmans bought the place in 1900 and added a frame Victorian farmhouse and some barns. The Parks and Wildlife Department acquired these buildings with the land and they are being preserved approximately as they would have looked when the Beckmans were living here in 1918 — without electricity, gas or plumbing. Park employees do routine farm chores here everyday, wearing 1918 clothes, cooking and cleaning and tending the cows, horses, sheep and chickens. The employees are not strangers to farm chores and part of their job is to explain to visitors what they are doing and why. They keep a garden and they cook and can the produce the way the Sauers and Beckmans did. Longhorn cattle and deer graze in fenced pastures nearby. A trip to the Sauer-Beckman farm is a special treat for young Texans and they should take their grandparents if possible.

The best time to visit here is during wildflower season in the spring. Lady Bird Johnson has seen to it that there are plenty of bluebonnets here. You might see Mrs. Johnson if you come August 27. The late president's birthday is celebrated here then.

For more information

You can get more information about the Lyndon B. Johnson State Historical Park by writing to the Superintendent, LBJ State Historical Park, Box 238, Stonewall, TX 78671.

Other places to see

Besides the Blanco and Pedernales Falls parks, you may want to see Fredericksburg, 15 miles west (numerous historic homes and buildings, German eating and drinking places and the Admiral Nimitz State Historical Park); Enchanted Rock State Natural Area, 30 miles northwest of LBJ Park on F.M. 965, north of Fredericksburg; and Johnson City, 16 miles east, where the National Park Service conducts tours of Lyndon Johnson's boyhood home and his grandfather's log cabin.

The Sauer-Beckman Farmstead in the Lyndon B. Johnson State Historical Park is complete with animals, vegetable garden and a cook in the kitchen.

ADMIRAL NIMITZ STATE HISTORICAL PARK

U.S. 290 in Fredericksburg in Gillespie County, 69 miles northwest of San Antonio. Entrance fee: adults $2, children $1

Fredericksburg is an old German town established on the edge of Comanche territory in 1846. The Nimitzes are an old German family. The first Texas Nimitz was Charles. He came from Bremen and arrived here with the first settlers. Charles established a hotel and married Sophie Mueller in 1848 and they raised a family. A grandson became one of the most distinguished military leaders of the twentieth century. This building might not have survived, had he not. It would not be what it is today, anyway. The external appearance is about what it was in the 1880s and inside is a first-class museum.

The oldest part of the Nimitz Hotel was built by Charles Nimitz in 1852. The building was enlarged a few years later and then a three-story addition resembling a steamboat was put on in the 1880s. The Nimitz Hotel was the principal place to stay at what was an important stop on the road from San Antonio to San Diego before the railroads came. Rutherford B. Hayes, Robert E. Lee, Ulysses S. Grant and Philip Sheridan all stopped here at various times.

Chester W. Nimitz was born about a block from his grandfather's hotel in 1885 when the hotel was a busy and popular place. Nimitz went to the U.S. Naval Academy and worked his way up to admiral. President Roosevelt named Admiral Nimitz commander in chief of the Pacific Fleet immediately after the Japanese attack on Pearl Harbor and he eventually commanded all American forces in the Pacific.

The Nimitz Hotel was declining while the admiral's star was rising. The steamboat addition was altered beyond recognition. The hotel closed in 1963. Some local people organized a foundation to buy the building and turn it into a museum memorializing the admiral. Admiral Nimitz approved the plan, but said he wanted the museum to be a memorial to all the men and women of all the American forces in the Pacific in World War II. The museum opened in 1967 as the Admiral Nimitz Center. Our armed forces and several foreign governments donated war relics. The Japanese built a garden behind the hotel after Admiral Nimitz died in 1966.

The legislature created a commission in 1970 to manage the museum and then in 1981 transferred the Nimitz Center to the Parks and Wildlife Department.

The original backers, in the meantime, raised money to restore the hotel

Opposite Right: Admiral Chester W. Nimitz engineered the ruin of Japan's military machine. But he was an admirer of one of the heros of Japan's earlier war with Russia. Nimitz helped get Admiral Heihachiro Togo's old flagship restored after the end of World War II.

Opposite Far Right: The Japanese returned the favor by building this garden on the grounds of the Nimitz Hotel in 1976. There is a replica of Admiral Togo's study in the garden.

building's exterior and renovate the interior. It is completely air conditioned now and filled with artifacts, mementos and photographs recalling the admiral's career and the war in the Pacific. The exhibits feature recorded comments by several of the admiral's contemporaries.

This park really occupies two sites. The hotel complex is right on Main Street. The History Walk of the Pacific War is a few blocks away. You can drive, but it is not too far to walk. The History Walk is a collection of guns and planes and tanks actually used in the Pacific War and gathered from various battlefields. Explanatory brochures are furnished and tape recordings explain the history of the exhibits.

For more information

You can get more information about the Admiral Nimitz State Historical Park or arrange for group tours by calling (512) 997-4379 or by writing the Superintendent at P.O. Box 777, Fredericksburg, TX 78624.

Other places to see

You probably will want to visit the Pioneer Museum and sample some of the German food and look at some of the old houses and buildings while you are in Fredericksburg.

Some other places you may want to visit in the area are Enchanted Rock State Natural Area (second biggest stone mountain in the country), 18 miles north of town on F.M. 965; Kerrville State Recreation Area, 27 miles southwest on U.S. 173; LBJ Ranch and Lyndon B. Johnson State Historical Park, 15 miles east on U.S. 290; and Lyndon Johnson's boyhood home and Sam Ealy Johnson cabin in Johnson City, 31 miles east of U.S. 290; and Pedernales Falls State Park, 14 miles east of Johnson City off Ranch Road 2766, Kerrville and Pedernales Falls both have full campgrounds. Enchanted Rock has only tent camping and primitive camping.

ENCHANTED ROCK STATE NATURAL AREA

18 miles north of Fredericksburg on F.M. 965, in Llano and Gillespie counties, 87 miles northwest of San Antonio. Entrance fee: $2 per car

Enchanted Rock is the biggest hunk of granite in Texas and the second biggest stone mountain in America. This park is a special treat for rock climbers and a big favorite with hikers.

Some internal upheaval a billion years ago shoved a mass of granite up into the earth's crust. The crust weathered away over the years and left five stone mountains exposed here. Enchanted Rock is the biggest one. All five are included in this park.

Enchanted Rock got its name because of Indian superstitions. The stone sparkles on moonlit nights when it is wet and the mountain makes noises some nights. There are cracks in the mountain. The granite expands on hot days and then contracts at night. There is sometimes enough movement to generate groaning noises along the cracks when the days are hot enough and the nights are cool enough.

The Indians did not know anything about expansion and contraction, so they made up stories to explain the noises and the night shine. The stories had to do mostly with unhappy deities. The Indians were convinced the mountain was haunted by angry gods or by the ghosts of people the gods were angry with.

Indians were aware of the big stone mountain thousands of years ago. The Spanish explorers evidently never came across it. There is no mention of it in their records. Anglo settlers first became aware of it in 1829 when Capt. Henry Brown reported seeing it while he was chasing Indians in the area.

A plaque on top of Enchanted Rock testifies that Ranger Capt. Jack Hays successfully fought off a band of Comanches here in 1841. Capt. Hays was on a roll at the time. He had discovered Sam Colt's revolver a couple of years earlier and he was more than a match for the Comanches.

Enchanted Rock was in private hands from the days of the republic until 1978. It was owned once by Samuel Maverick of San Antonio. It was operated as a private resort for 30 years until the Parks and Wildlife Department and the Nature Conservancy bought it in 1978. The department has improved the hiking trails and put in modern restrooms, but the development has been deliberately limited to preserve as much of the wilderness atmosphere as possible.

There are 62 picnic sites here and 106 camping sites. Sixty of the camping sites are primitive sites on the hiking trails. The other 46 are grouped near the park headquarters. Each of these sites has a table and a grill. Some have shade shelters.

The Enchanted Rock State Natural Area was closed for more than a year while the Parks and Wildlife Department was making improvements, including this shelter at the head of the trail to the summit of Enchanted Rock. The park reopened in March, 1984.

All of them are near water taps and restrooms. The campsites are $4 a night. There are no hookups and no plans for any. RV's and trailers are not allowed.

The park has two playgrounds and a group picnic shelter which rents for $8 a day for groups up to 25. The rent is $16 a day for bigger groups. The group shelter has electricity, water, grill and restrooms. There is no kitchen.

The most popular hiking trail is the one to the top of Enchanted Rock. It is moderately strenuous for the average park visitor. Real rock climbers would not bother with it. The summit of Enchanted Rock is 400 feet above the surrounding countryside. This area is especially pretty in the spring when wildflowers bloom among the granite boulders.

For more information

The address for reservations or more information about Enchanted Rock State Natural Area is Rt. 4, Box 170, Fredericksburg, TX 78624. The phone number is (915) 247-3903.

Other places to see

Other places to visit nearby are Inks Lake State Park, 46 miles northeast on Park Road 4 off F.M. 2341, west of Burnet; Longhorn Cavern State Park, 52 miles northeast on Park Road 4 off F.M. 2341; Fredericksburg and the Admiral Nimitz State Historical Park, 18 miles south on F.M. 965; and LBJ Ranch and Lyndon B. Johnson State Historical Park at Stonewall, 34 miles southeast on U.S. 290.

KERRVILLE STATE RECREATION AREA

On U.S. 173, 3 miles southeast of Kerrville in Kerr County, 63 miles northwest of San Antonio. Entrance fee: $2 per car

This is one of the parks developed during the Great Depression with the help of the CCC and the National Park Service, as much to create jobs as to create recreation areas. The National Park Service drew the plans and the CCC did the work after the city of Kerrville donated this 500 acres in 1934. The land was valued at $25,000 at the time. Ask your real estate broker what 500 acres on the Guadalupe River is worth now.

This park is divided into two sections of unequal size. The smaller section is between Highway 173 and a small lake created by a dam on the river at the lower end of the park. The larger section is on the opposite side of Highway 173. It is hilly with some timber and a large part of it has been left in its natural state.

A number of retired people from bigger cities live in the hills around Kerrville. Some of them had their first experience with Hill Country living in this park.

Most of the 30 picnic sites are in the lake side unit. Both units have extensive campgrounds. The lake side unit has eight screened shelters on the lake for $8 a night, 20 campsites with water and electricity for $6 a night and 16 campsites with water for $4 a night. The campsites all have tables and grills. The restrooms have showers. This unit has one recreation hall accommodating up to 55 people for $40 a day or $70 overnight.

A group picnic area is for rent in the lake side unit at $16 a day. It has eight tables. The lake side unit has a playground, a boat ramp, a lighted fishing pier and an amphitheater. One section of the lake is designated for swimming, but there are no lifeguards.

The hill side unit has eight screened shelters for rent at $8; 20 trailer campsites with water, sewer connections, electricity, table and grill at $7; 15 sites with water, electricity, table and grill at $6; and 49 sites with water, table and grill at $4. A group camping area in this unit offers a screened dining hall and seven screened shelters. The dining hall has a kitchen, tables and benches. It rents for $50 plus $8 a night for each of the screened shelters. The group picnic site here is similar to the one in the lake side unit. It rents for $16 a day.

There are three individual picnic sites in this unit, one playground, and seven miles of hiking trails. Hikers often see white-tail deer along the trails. There are

The lake side unit of the Kerrville State Recreation Area has 8 screened shelters overlooking the little lake formed by a dam on the Guadalupe River.

wild turkeys, armadillos and jackrabbits, too. Many varieties of birds are seen here, including the one that was the special favorite of the late J. Frank Dobie — the paisano, or chaparral, also known as the road-runner.

This is a popular park, usually at its prettiest during wildflower season in the spring. You should make reservations, especially in the summer.

For more information

The address is 2385 Bandera Highway, Kerrville, TX 78028. The phone number is (512) 257-5392.

Other places to see

Other interesting places you may want to visit are Kerrville (the Schreiner home and the Cowboy Art Museum); Fredericksburg, 23 miles northeast (Admiral Nimitz State Historical Park, historic buildings and German eating and drinking places); Stonewall, 50 miles northeast (LBJ Ranch and Lyndon B. Johnson State Historical Park); Bandera, 23 miles south (Frontier Times Museum); and Lost Maples State Natural Area, 40 miles southwest on Ranch Road 187 north of Vanderpool.

This area has some of the nicest scenery in the state. A quick way to see some of it is to take Highway 173 into Kerrville, and then go west on State Highway 39 along the Guadalupe to Hunt, and farther if you have time.

The Y.O. Ranch, 14 miles west of Mountain Home about 36 miles from the Kerrville Park, is one of the most famous guest ranches in this dude ranch country. The Y.O. is owned by the pioneer Schreiner family of Kerrville.

HILL COUNTRY STATE NATURAL AREA

At the west end of F.M. 1077, 10½ miles southwest of Bandera in Bandera and Medina counties, 60 miles west of San Antonio. No fees

This park is not currently scheduled for development. It is an old ranch given to the Parks and Wildlife Department by Louise Merrick. The 4,750 acres here are being allowed to return to their natural state. The only camping allowed is primitive camping. There are no amenities and no utilities. There is no water except at the trailhead near the headquarters. What is in the creeks and ponds on the property is not fit for drinking.

Campers must bring everything they need. No fires are allowed; any cooking has to be done on stoves using containerized fuel. There is one wilderness trail.

The people attracted to this park so far have been mostly hikers and riders. Several organized riding groups have been using the park for weekend events. Not many state parks have room for riding events. This park has little else so far.

It is not easy to find the Hill Country State Natural Area. The access roads have no signs. Don't ask people in Bandera where F.M. 1077 is. They do not know it by that name. The road is usually called the Dixie Dude Ranch Road here. It runs west from U.S. 173 about a half mile south of the courthouse square in Bandera. The park is well beyond the end of the pavement.

This is the heart of dude ranch country. You will pass the Dixie Dude Ranch on your right before you reach the Hill Country State Natural Area. You might want to talk to the people at this dude ranch if you want to visit this park and don't feel up to primitive camping. They take in boarders.

For more information

You can get more information about the Hill Country State Natural Area from the Superintendent at Rt. 1, Box 601, Bandera, TX 78003. The phone number is (512) 796-4413.

Other places to see

Other places nearby are Bandera (Frontier Times Museum); Kerrville State Recreation Area, 34 miles north; Castroville and the Landmark Inn State Historical Site, 42 miles southeast; and Lost Maples State Natural Area, 48 miles west on Ranch Road 187 north of Vanderpool.

Opposite Top: The Hill Country State Natural Area is at the dead-end of a country road southwest of Bandera.

Opposite Bottom: There are no utilities and no conveniences in the Hill Country State Natural Area, but riding groups have discovered it. There are no fees here, but the superintendent does like to have advance notice when groups are coming. The office is closed Tuesdays and Wednesdays. You will need insect repellent in the summer.

LOST MAPLES STATE NATURAL AREA

On Ranch Road 187, 4 miles north of Vanderpool in Bandera County, 86 miles northwest of San Antonio. Entrance fee: $2 per car.

This park has had the development the Hill Country Natural Area has yet to get. It is less development than the state parks and state recreation areas get. There are no electric outlets at the campsites and no sewer connections. There are only primitive campsites and sites with water, table and grill. There are restrooms with showers in the main campground and primitive toilets on the trails and at the primitive campgrounds. No campfires are allowed. Cooking must be done on stoves using containerized fuel. The idea is to disturb the natural environment as little as possible; so there probably never will be trailer hookups here.

The main attraction at this park in the Sabinal River canyon is the stand of bigtooth maple trees. It is thought that these trees grew in many parts of Texas in the distant past when the climate was wetter. They survive now only in isolated and protected spots like this canyon. Most visitors come here in the fall when the maples are changing color. The trees can be very spectacular in early November if there has been enough rain and enough sunshine and if the fall nights are cool enough. The colors are less spectacular when these conditions are not present. You can call a toll-free number to find out whether the trees are looking great or only so-so. The number is (800) 792-1112. This service is available from October through November.

Hikers and birdwatchers will enjoy this park any time of year. The hills, the limestone canyons here at the edge of the Edwards Plateau, and the river have their own beauty year-round. Golden-cheeked warblers, canyon wrens, black-capped vireos and green kingfishers nest here. Golden eagles and bald eagles are seen here in the winter months. White-tail deer are common. There are foxes, bobcats and mountain lions in the hills.

The park has a short nature trail along the river canyon near the main visitor parking area. This trail is not difficult and it puts hikers close to some of the maples. There are 10 miles of rougher trails offering views of other maples most visitors never see in Hale's Hollow and along Can Creek.

Eight primitive camping areas dot the hiking trails. The main campground near the park entrance has 30 campsites with water, table and grill. All the campsites in this park are $4 a night. There are 20 picnic sites near the trailhead.

For more information

The address for reservations or more information is Lost Maples State Natural Area, Station C Route, Vanderpool, TX 78885. The phone number is (512) 966-3413.

Other places to see

One of the most scenic drives you will find in Texas is near here. It is Ranch Road 337 between Medina and Camp Wood. A campground with more conveniences is located just 35 miles southwest of here at Garner State Park on U.S. 83, 10 miles south of Leakey (prounced Lakey).

October certainly is the best time to visit Lost Maples State Natural Area. But this park in the Sabinal River canyon is pleasant and pretty anytime. The park covers 2,200 acres. Visitors are cautioned not to disturb any plants or carry away any rocks.

GARNER STATE PARK

31 miles north of Uvalde on U.S. 83 in Uvalde County, 114 miles west of San Antonio. Entrance fee: $2 per car

This park attracts more overnight visitors than any other park in the state system, year after year. It is popular with families and students, and many hunters stay here during deer season. Some students almost made a cult of it in the 60s. This is the only park with its own song. The Triumphs recorded it at the Crazy Cajun Studios in Houston and "Garner State Park" got a big play on the juke box here in the middle 1960s. People knowledgeable about such things say it was a "surfer's stomp." B. J. Thomas was one of the Triumphs when the group recorded this song.

Anyone craving solitude will not find it here. Garner is especially crowded on summer weekends. The campsites are usually all occupied then and the picnic areas are overflowing. Many picnickers bring their own grills and chairs, knowing all the tables will be taken. You are sure to spend some time listening to somebody else's music if you come to Garner.

Something I have observed in the parks, generally, is especially observable here. The vast majority of campers are Caucasians. More than half of the picnickers are Hispanic, and there are very few Blacks camping or picnicking. I cannot explain it. I am only reporting it.

The Parks and Wildlife Department is experimenting with a computerized reservation system. It is being tried at Garner because of the volume of reservations here. Reservations for the whole system may be put on a central computer if the experiment works out. Then you will be able to make reservations for a series of stops across the state with one call, just like Holiday Inn does it.

There is a short hiking trail here, but the main attraction is the Frio River. Sometimes it seems half the people in the park are in the water, swimming or rafting or riding in rented pedal boats. The river is fed by springs in the limestone hills along the edge of the Edwards Plateau. The water usually is fresh and cool. A small dam at the lower end of the park creates a shallow lake.

The Frio is one of our more picturesque rivers. The river canyon is lined with cypress, elm, oak and pecan trees. Much of the park is carpeted with wildflowers in the spring. Deer often graze in the park.

Uvalde County bought the land here in 1935 and gave it to the Parks Board in 1936, at the time the National Park Service and the CCC were building parks around the country to make work for the unemployed. Uvalde County probably did not have to do a lot of lobbying in Washington. Uvalde resident John Nance Garner was vice president at the time. He was the first native Texan to be elected

Garner State Park is the most popular camping park in the state system. It is always crowded with day visitors on summer weekends.

to national office. He put Uvalde on the map. His constituents named this park for him. The CCC built the original improvements including 14 cabins.

Garner has a wide range of accommodations for campers. There are 211 campsites with grills and water at $4 a night; 146 sites with grills, water and electricity at $6 a night; 40 screened shelters at $8 a night; and 18 cabins sleeping up to six people each. The cabins rent for $18 a night for the first one or two people, with an additional charge of $4 a night for each additional adult and $1 a night for each additional child. Linens and towels are furnished. Blankets, dishes and utensils are not.

The group shelter here has a dining hall and five stone shelters with bunks and mattresses but no linens. The dining hall has a kitchen with range, refrigerator and freezer. This combination can accommodate up to 40 people overnight for a fee of $100. The dining hall can be rented by itself when there is no group encamped. The fee for the hall alone is $50.

The park also has a group picnic shelter with kitchen, stove and refrigerator. It has 12 tables and can seat up to 75 people. It is for day use only and rents for $50. There are 20 individual picnic sites in the park, a grocery store, restaurant, laundromat and dance pavillion.

For more information

You can make reservations or get more information about Garner State Park by writing the Superintendent at Concan, TX 78838. The phone number is (512) 232-6132.

Other places to see

You may want to see Lost Maples State Natural Area (30 miles northeast on Ranch Road 187, 4 miles north of Vanderpool), Uvalde and the Garner Memorial Museum.

Ranch Road 337 between Medina and Leakey and State Highway 55 between Uvalde and Rock Springs are two of the more scenic drives in Texas.

LANDMARK INN STATE HISTORIC SITE

On U.S. 90 in Castroville in Medina County, 20 miles west of San Antonio.
Fees: adults $1, children 25¢

This old hotel is an antique of the best kind; it is useful and being used. The Landmark Inn has rooms for travelers and it is open for tours, too. The tours are $1 for adults and 25 cents for children. The tour includes a walk around the grounds and through the ruined mill on the river bank.

The Landmark Inn has been on the south bank of the Medina River for a long time. Castroville was established by Henri Castro in 1844 and the original settlers were from Alsace-Lorraine. Cesar Monod had his home and a store here. Later owners expanded the building and started renting rooms to travelers. It was called the Vance Hotel for a time. A grist mill was added in the 1850s and it was expanded to saw lumber and gin cotton.

Jordan Lawler and his sister Ruth bought the property in 1925. Lawler converted the mill to a generator and became the original supplier of electricity to the city of Castroville. The Lawlers reopened the hotel during World War II. They gave it the name Landmark Inn.

Ruth Lawler gave the property to the state in 1974 after Jordan died. She still lives in a house on the property and she sometimes visits with hotel guests. The Parks and Wildlife Department has restored the inn and furnished it in country style. It has become a very popular stopping place.

There are just eight rooms for rent. Most of them have private baths. The rates are $20 for a single, $24 for a double, plus $1 for each child, aged 6-12. The Landmark Inn has no dining room, but there are several eating places nearby.

For more information

The address for more information or reservations is Park Manager, Landmark Inn State Historic Site, P.O. Box 577, Castroville, TX 78009. The phone number is (512) 538-2133.

Other places to see

Nearly everything in Castroville is interesting. You probably will want to drive along every street. Many of the homes and buildings built by the original Alsatian settlers are still here. Especially notable are the St. Louis Catholic Church buildings and the old Moye Academy building now being used as a convent.

The nearest state park with a campground is Guadalupe River State Park, 57 miles northeast on State Highway 46 between U.S. 281 and Boerne (pronounced "Bernie").

Texas has a growing number of country inns. Only one is operated by the Parks and Wildlife Department. It is the Landmark Inn in picturesque Castroville.

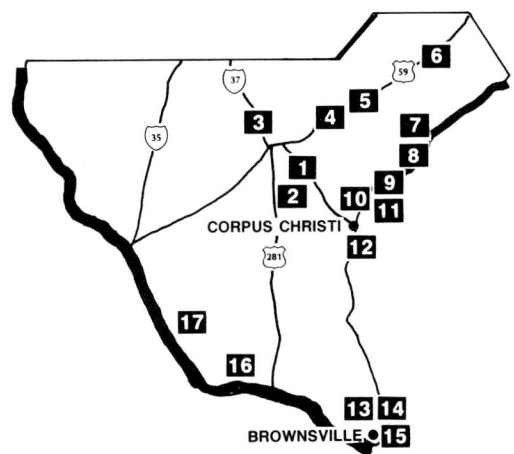

1. Lake Corpus Christi State Recreation Area
2. Lipantilan State Historic Site
3. Tips State Recreation Area
4. Goliad State Historical Park
5. Fannin Battleground State Historic Site
6. Lake Texana State Recreation Area
7. Port Lavaca State Fishing Pier
8. Matagorda Island State Park and Wildlife Management Area
9. Copano Bay State Fishing Pier
10. Fulton Mansion State Historic Structure
11. Goose Island State Recreation Area
12. Mustang Island State Park
13. Port Isabel Lighthouse Historic Structure
14. Queen Isabella State Fishing Pier
15. Brazos Island State Recreation Area
16. Bentsen-Rio Grande Valley State Park
17. Falcon State Recreation Area

REGION VI
PARKS IN SOUTH TEXAS

Twelve of the state parks in this area are within easy driving distance of Corpus Christi. The other five are at the southern tip of the state. Three new parks are planned in the lower valley.

The parks near Corpus Christi could serve as an example of the variety available in state parks in Texas. There are two on freshwater lakes and two on the beach. There is a revolutionary battleground, an old Spanish mission and a historic mansion.

Corpus Christi is the biggest city in this section of the state. The parks are listed in the order you would encounter them if you drove from Corpus Christi up the Nueces and then swung around the area clockwise. You would want to see Corpus Christi first, of course. The numbers are simply numbers and not ratings. My favorite park in this area is Goose Island State Recreation Area.

Parks Under Development

There are three parks in various stages of development in this region:

Arroyo Colorado Park, on the Arroyo Colorado in Cameron and Willacy counties, is near the town of Arroyo and the Laguna Atascosa National Wildlife Refuge. The site is 687 acres. The Parks and Wildlife Department bought 472 acres in 1979 for about $800,000, and leased 178 acres. Thirty-seven acres were donated. This is South Texas brushland, chapparral country.

Choke Canyon Park, near Three Rivers in Live Oak and McMullen counties, covers 32,000 acres. The Parks and Wildlife Department leased the land in 1981 from the federal government. The park will include and make use of some of the buildings in the old town of Calliham. The Bureau of Reclamation of the Department of the Interior relocated the town of Calliham before it started work on the Choke Canyon Dam on the Frio River here.

Resaca de Palma Park, on the Resaca de Palma in Cameron County, near Olmito, covers 1,100 acres of brushland. The Parks and Wildlife Department bought the site in 1978 for about $2 million. It is in the same area but does not include the Resaca de la Palma Battleground, where Zachary Taylor's U.S. troops and Mexican soldiers fought one of the first battles of the Mexican War in May, 1846. *Resaca* is the Spanish word for an ox-bow lake, left behind when a river changes course. The Rio Grande has changed courses many times. Resacas are common in the Valley.

LAKE CORPUS CHRISTI STATE RECREATION AREA

Off F.M. 1068, 6 miles southwest of Mathis in San Patricio County, 35 miles north of Corpus Christi. Entrance fee: $2 per car

There is no other place in Texas where a state park on a freshwater lake is this close to the beach. Fishermen in Corpus Christi have a lot of choices.

The city of Corpus Christi created this lake in the early 1930s by damming the Nueces River to get a water supply. It is a big lake, covering 21,000 acres with 200 miles of shore line. The park is at the lower end of the lake in a protected cove. The old Parks Board leased this 350 acres from the city of Corpus Christi in 1934 for 99 years. The CCC built the original improvements, including a bathhouse, two boathouses, a dock and a concession building with the usual dance terrace.

The park has a swimming beach with no lifeguards. There are boat ramps and fishing piers and fish-cleaning tables. Fishermen get channel catfish, yellow catfish, blue catfish, bass, perch and crappie here. Water skiing and sailing are also popular. The park has a marina and a park store with gasoline, food and bait for sale. The concessionaire rents small fishing boats and pedal boats.

Whitewing doves are among the birds regularly seen in this park. The bird checklist for Lake Corpus Christi includes more than 300 species. The birds are not attracted by trees here. This is what is called chaparral country. The vegetation is mostly brush and mesquite.

Lake Corpus Christi Recreation Area has 25 screened shelters for rent at $8 a night. The 25 campsites with full hookups — water, electricity and sewer connections — are $7 a night. There are 23 sites with water and electricity for $6 a night and 60 primitive sites for $4 a night. Restrooms in the camping areas have showers. There is also a primitive camping area. The park has 137 individual picnic sites and one group picnic shelter accommodating up to 75 people. The group shelter rents for $8 a day for groups up to 25. Groups of 26 to 100 pay $16.

The nature trail and playground are well used. This is a popular park.

For more information

You can make reservations or get more information by writing the Superintendent, Lake Corpus Christi State Recreation Area, Box 1167, Mathis, TX 78368. The phone number is (512) 547-2635.

Other places to see

Some other places you may want to see while you are in this area are Corpus Christi and Padre Island, 35 miles southeast, and the King Ranch at Kingsville, 43 miles south. The main gate is on State Highway 141 and tourists are welcome to drive through part of this famous property.

The vegetation around Lake Corpus Christi is not lush. This is brush and mesquite country. The park has two fishing piers. The concessionaire rents small boats and canoes.

LIPANTILAN STATE HISTORIC SITE

On County Road 101, east of Orange Grove in Nueces County, 31 miles northwest of Corpus Christi. No fee

Some of the early skirmishes of the Texas Revolution occurred here in November, 1835. Texans had won an engagement at Gonzales the month before. Texans were in San Antonio beseiging the Alamo. There had been no Declaration of Independence yet, but the war was beginning.

Texas volunteers led by Ira Westover seized a small mud fort from the Mexican garrison at this location on November 4. The fort had been established in 1831 on the site of a Lipan Apache village. The Mexicans called the fort Lipantilan. It still had that name after the revolution when a band of Texans commanded by James Davis fought off a Mexican attack in 1842. Destiny was finished with Lipantilan. All traces of the fort disappeared long ago.

The pioneer Bluntzer family donated this five-acre site to the state in 1937, asking that it be designated the J. C. Bluntzer Memorial Lipantilan Park. The State Board of Control passed the land to the State Parks Board in 1949. No improvements have been made beyond a few picnic tables. Lipantilan appears on the list of state parks and carries a park symbol on the maps issued by the Department of Highways and Public Transportation, but it is not worth going out of your way to see. It is not easy to find, either, but if you are determined, you can take F.M. 624 southeast from Orange Grove, turn north onto State Highway 70, go 3½ miles and turn east on County Road 58. County Road 101 branches off County Road 58. Lipantilan is at the dead end of County Road 101.

TIPS STATE RECREATION AREA

Off State Highway 72 just west of Three Rivers in Live Oak County, 76 miles northwest of Corpus Christi. No fee

The Parks and Wildlife Department does not operate this park, but it is one of the oldest in the state. This 31 acres on the Frio River was donated to the state in 1925 before the original Parks Board was established. It was transferred to the Parks Board in 1935. The board put in some picnic tables and some other improvements, but the park has been leased for many years to the city of Three Rivers. It is used mostly by local people for picnicking and fishing.

Top: Tips State Park is leased to the city of Three Rivers. It is a very small picnic area with a boat ramp on the Frio River on the western edge of Three Rivers. It is neither very attractive nor very well maintained.

Opposite: There is little at the Lipantilan State Historic Site today except a granite marker. There was a small Mexican fort here in colonial days and it was occupied by Texans briefly after the revolution.

GOLIAD STATE HISTORICAL PARK

On U.S. 183, ¼ mile south of Goliad in Goliad County, 70 miles north of Corpus Christi. Entrance fee: $2 per car

Some of the important events of the Texas Revolution happened near this park. The main feature of the park is the Mission Espiritu Santo. The mission was already old at the time of the revolution.

The Spanish originally established Nuestra Senora del Espiritu Santo de Zuniga Mission on the coast in 1722. That was shortly after the French explorer LaSalle had made his accidental landing on the Texas coast. The Spanish thought it was necessary to make some show of their claim to the territory. Their usual way of doing that was to set up a mission and a presidio to guard the mission.

The French never came back. The Spanish moved the mission and presidio from the bay to near Victoria in 1726 and moved them again to this site on the San Antonio River in 1749. The name had been inspired by the original location next to the bay. The Spanish called it Bahia del Espiritu Santo. The mission and the presidio were commonly called "La Bahia" and that name stayed with the mission and presidio through the moves to Victoria and Goliad. La Bahia was one of the most successful Spanish missions. The Presidio La Bahia was one of the major seats of Spanish and Mexican authority in colonial days. One of the most important roads in the days when Anglo settlers were first being admitted to Texas was La Bahia Road from Nacogdoches to Goliad.

The mission was closed in 1829. The presidio became a town and an important one. Roads were bad. Travel was easier by water. Mexican Gen. Martin Perfecto de Cos came to Texas from Matamoros by water in the fall of 1835. Texans were preparing for war. Cos wanted to head them off. He brought a small army in through Copano Bay to Goliad and left some supplies here and a few troops. Cos and most of the army went on to San Antonio to show the flag. Cos did not know at the time that the first battle of the revolution was being fought while he was stopping here at Goliad. Settlers and volunteers won a skirmish with Mexican troops at Gonzales on October 2. Some Texans marched on to San Antonio. Others marched on Goliad. They captured the old presidio and Cos's supplies. The Mexican general had a very uncomfortable time in San Antonio, cut off from supplies and reinforcements. Cos surrendered the city and the Alamo December 9. Texans remained in possession of the Alamo until March 6, 1836, when Santa Anna took it back.

Texans remained in possession of Goliad until March 19. Col. James Fannin was in command at the presidio by that time. Sam Houston ordered Fannin to retreat to Victoria after the Alamo fell. Fannin delayed obeying the order because he had some of his troops out in the boondocks trying to help civilians get out of the way of the advancing Mexicans. It was too late when he finally pulled out of Goliad. Gen. Jose Urrea and 1,000 Mexicans were on his heels. They fought a battle a few miles east of here. Fannin was hopelessly outgunned and he surrendered. He and his troops were marched back to Goliad and executed in an episode that provoked as much anger among Texans as the massacre at the Alamo. The remains of Fannin and his men are buried near the presidio. The cemetery is officially part of the Goliad State Historical Park. The presidio, where most of the action occurred, is not part of the park, but it is open to visitors. The presidio

The Spanish customarily built a fortress or presidio wherever they built a mission. The Presidio La Bahia is less than a mile from the Mission Bahia. Architect Raiford Stripling restored the presidio in the 1960s. Kathryn Stoner O'Connor paid the bills. The presidio is not part of the park. The Catholic church owns it but it is open to visitors.

and the mission both were neglected for years and allowed to fall into ruins.

The city of Goliad put the mission back together in 1848 and used it as a public school for a while. It was occupied by a private college for a time after that. The city of Goliad and Goliad County offered the mission site to the state as a park in 1931. The legislature accepted the offer and put the mission in the hands of the State Board of Control. There was no Parks Board yet. The people of Goliad started restoring the mission in collaboration with the CCC, WPA and the National Park Service. The Parks Board became responsible for the property in 1949. The Parks and Wildlife Department located and installed some authentic furnishings and fixtures. Visitors can tour the mission complex. Exhibits in the visitor center explain some of the mission's history.

This park also has an assortment of campsites, a swimming pool and a hiking trail along the San Antonio River. The park covers 186 acres on both sides of U.S. 183. There are 41 picnic sites; ten campsites with water, table and grill for $4 a night; 20 sites with water, electricity, table and grill for $6 a night; and 20 sites with water, electricity, sewer connections, table and grill for $7 a night. Five screened shelters rent for $8 a night and a group shelter accommodating up to 75 people rents for $50 a day.

This park has two other outposts besides the Fannin cemetery. There was another mission a few miles west of here called Nuestra Senora del Rosario. Nothing is left but some rubble and a marker, but the site is part of this park. So is a small house right outside the presidio. This house was the birthplace of the Mexican hero, Ignacio Zaragoza. He won the 1862 battle with the French that Mexicans still celebrate on Cinco de Mayo (May 5).

The Presidio La Bahia is just south of this park off U.S. 183 on the other side of the San Antonio River. It was restored for the Catholic Church in the 1960s by Kathryn Stoner O'Connor.

For more information

You can write the Superintendent, Goliad State Historical Park, Box 727, Goliad, TX 77963 or call (512) 645-3405 for reservations or more information about this park.

Other places to see

The battleground where Fannin and Urrea fought the Battle of Coleto Creek is off U.S. 59, 9 miles east of Goliad. It is a state historic site. The city of Victoria is just 25 miles east. The Aransas National Wildlife Refuge (where the whooping cranes winter), Goose Island State Recreation Area and the Fulton Mansion Historic Structure are little more than an hour's drive south of here.

Col. James Fannin and his little army fought and then surrendered here to a large Mexican force commanded by Gen. Jose Urrea in March, 1836. Fannin and his men were later executed. The granite monument is a memorial to them. The building behind the marker is a picnic pavilion. The Fannin Battleground State Historic Site covers only 10 acres.

FANNIN BATTLEGROUND STATE HISTORIC SITE

Off U.S. 59, 9 miles east of Goliad in Goliad County, 79 miles north of Corpus Christi. No fee

This is one of our oldest parks. The owners gave the site to the state in 1913 because they thought it was too significant not to be preserved. This is the place Col. James Fannin chose to make his stand against a superior Mexican force he could not elude.

Fannin studied a couple of years at the U.S. Military Academy before he came to Texas in 1834. He became a slave trader and an agitator for Texas independence. He took part in the Battle of Gonzales October 2, 1835. Fannin was organizing an expedition against Matamoros when word reached Texas that Santa Anna was bringing an army up from Mexico to put an end to the rebellion.

The record suggests that Col. Fannin was indecisive and irresolute. He was the ranking officer in this area and he led his men to believe that he was going to defend Goliad. He gave the presidio the name "Fort Defiance." Fannin received orders from Sam Houston on March 12 to go to the aid of Col. Travis at the Alamo. Communications were so poor that Houston did not know when he sent the order that the Alamo had fallen two days earlier. Fannin did not know, either, that it

was too late to help Travis. But he was still at Goliad getting organized on March 13 when he received another order Houston wrote after he learned of the fall of the Alamo. Houston ordered Fannin to fall back to Victoria with as much artillery as could be moved expeditiously. The rest of the heavy weapons were to be dumped in the San Antonio River. Fannin had some of his troops and equipment out on scouting and rescue missions. He was not ready to leave the presidio until March 19. He tried to take all his cannon with him and could not move fast enough. The Mexicans caught up with him here on the prairie. Fannin and his men were outnumbered, but they put up a good fight and the issue was unresolved when night fell on the 19th. Mexican commander Jose Urrea brought up reinforcements and artillery during the night. Fannin had 60 wounded men and no way to move them. He had no food and no water. He accepted Urrea's offer to discuss surrender and he eventually did surrender on March 20.

About 400 prisoners were marched back to the presidio at Goliad. Fannin and most of the others were marched out and shot one week later. Fannin had tried to negotiate a written guarantee that his troops would only be deported. Gen. Urrea could not promise that, but he did promise to recommend that course to Santa Anna. But he apparently reported to Santa Anna only that the prisoners were at the disposal of the Supreme Mexican Government. The government had issued orders earlier that all foreigners captured with arms on Mexican territory were to be shot. Santa Anna sent word that the prisoners were to be executed. Gen. Urrea had moved on eastward by that time. The subordinate left in command of the presidio carried out the order; so the blame for the massacre cannot be put directly upon Urrea. But that is where Santa Anna put it the first time he was called to account. Sam Houston raised the question during his first discussion with the Mexican leader on the battlefield at San Jacinto on April 22. Santa Anna claimed to be surprised that Urrea had ever led Fannin to believe he would recommend clemency. He said he never heard about it and promised to take it up with Urrea at the first opportunity.

The battle fought here is referred to in most history books as the Battle of Coleto Creek. The principal feature of this little park is a granite marker memorializing the battle and the victims of the Goliad massacre. There are three individual picnic tables and a small pavillion with 10 tables. There is no campground.

For more information

You can get more information by writing the Superintendent, Fannin Battleground State Historic Site, Fannin, TX 77960. The phone number is (512) 645-2020.

Other places to see

Other places close by are the city of Victoria, 25 miles northeast; Goliad State Historial Park and Presidio La Bahia, 9 miles southwest;and the Aransas Wildlife Refuge at Austwell, 50 miles southeast.

LAKE TEXANA STATE RECREATION AREA

Off State Highway 111, 6½ miles southwest of Edna in Jackson County, 116 miles northeast of Corpus Christi. Entrance fee: $2 per car

This is a new park on a new lake. The Lavaca-Navidad River Authority created the lake in 1980 by damming the Navidad River at Palmetto Bend. The Parks and Wildlife Department is leasing the 575 acres here from the River Authority.

Lake Texana has been stocked with large-mouth bass and striped bass. Fishermen get a lot of crappie here, too. There are two boat ramps. Two of the three fishing piers are lighted. Fishing is the big attraction, but many skiiers come here, too. The lake is big enough for almost any kind of boat. Swimming is at your own risk; there are no lifeguards.

The lake and the park are on the Coastal Plain, but there are substantial stands of oak, elm and pecan trees here.

There are two campgrounds in this park and a playground. One campground has 55 campsites with water, table and grill for $4 a night. The other campground has 86 sites with water, electricity, table and grill for $6 a night. The restrooms in the camping areas have showers.

There are 70 individual picnic sites on the lake shore. The picnic pavilion here

Lake Texana is a popular fishing resort. *Texas Fisherman* editor Larry Bozka says it is one of the premier catfish lakes in the state and the best months are February through April.

can accommodate up to 100 people. It rents for $8 a day for groups up to 25 and $16 a day for larger groups.

This lake and this park are named for an extinct town. Dr. F. F. Wells established a town in 1832 near the junction of the Navidad and Lavaca rivers, south of here. Texas was Mexican territory then. One of Mexico's heroes was a general named Santa Anna. Dr. Wells named his town Santa Anna. The name was changed to Texana in 1835 when it was apparent that Santa Anna and Texas did not have much in common. Texana was the first county seat when Jackson County was created. The town had a newspaper, regular steamship service and several business houses in 1880. The people and the government moved to the new town of Edna after the New York, Texas and Mexican Railroad laid tracks through here in 1883. Texana declined and died. There is only a marker at the site.

There are eight public boat ramps around this lake besides the ramps in the park. The River Authority has a large campground and marina on the opposite side of Highway 111 from the park. It is operated by a concessionaire. The Parks and Wildlife Department limits campers to 14 consecutive days. Campers wanting to stay longer in Lake Texana Park sometimes move across the road to the Brackenridge Campground for a couple of days and then move back into the park. The Brackenridge Campground is on the site of the plantation established in the 1850s by John and Isabella Brackenridge. They were the parents of the San Antonio philanthropist, George Brackenridge.

For more information

The address for more information about Lake Texana State Park or for reservations is Superintendent, Box 666, Edna, TX 77957. The phone number is (512) 782-5718.

Other places to see

Some other places to see in this area are the city of Victoria, 31 miles southwest; Port O'Connor, 48 miles south (gateway to Matagorda Island Park); and Indianola, 42 miles south (once an important port, completely destroyed by hurricanes in the late 1800s. LaSalle landed near here in 1685. La Bahia Mission and Presidio were near here originally because of LaSalle).

The Port Lavaca State Fishing Pier is lighted at night. Panfishing with dead bait is good here throughtout the summer and fall.

PORT LAVACA STATE FISHING PIER

On State Highway 35 at Lavaca Bay, 75 miles northeast of Corpus Christi in Calhoun County. Fee: $1 per rod

The Parks and Wildlife Department has more than a hundred fishing piers in its various parks. There are three fishing piers that are nothing but fishing piers. All three are on saltwater. All three are old bridges. All three are in this part of the state.

This fishing pier is part of the old Highway 35 bridge across Lavaca Bay. The highway department built a new bridge right alongside the old one several years ago. The Parks and Wildlife Department claimed the old one for fishermen.

Nothing is left now but a stub at the Port Lavaca end. It is 3,200 feet long; so it will hold a lot of fishermen. The pier is operated by a concessionaire. The fishing fee is $1 per rod or pole or thrownet for 24 hours. The concessionaire also sells bait and fishing equipment.

The city of Port Lavaca has a small park on the old highway leading to the pier. Camping sites and hookups are available for a fee, right on the water next to the pier.

For more information

You can write to the concessionaire at 114 Linnville, Port Lavaca, TX 77979 for more information. The phone number at the concession stand is (512) 552-4667.

Other places to see

Other places in the area you might want to see are Lake Texana State Park, 30 miles north off State Highway 111 on the west bank of Lake Texana; Indianola, 19 miles south (site of a thriving port wiped out by hurricanes in the late 1800s); Port O'Connor and Matagorda Island State Park, 30 miles south; and Austwell and the Aransas Wildlife Refuge, 32 miles southeast.

MATAGORDA ISLAND STATE PARK AND WILDLIFE MANAGEMENT AREA

Accessible only by boat, headquarters in Port O'Connor on State Highway 185 in Calhoun County, 102 miles northeast of Corpus Christi. No entrance fee.

The Army Air Corps was training bomber crews at Ellington Air Field and other Texas bases in World War II. The trainees needed some place to drop their bombs. Nothing was going on here; so the government bought the northern two-thirds of Matagorda Island and used it for a bombing range. There was a landing strip and a small base, but most of the land was used for target practice. Many of the craters are still visible.

The Army Air Corps became the Air Force and the bombers continued to use the range here. It also became a hunting resort for Air Force brass. The government and conservationists agonized for years over what should be done with the property. They had grave reservations about whether an agency of the state could be trusted with it.

The state and federal people eventually agreed in 1983 that the Parks and Wildlife Department could assume jurisdiction over the 43,893 acres here with the understanding that only 7,325 acres would be a park and the rest would be a wildlife management area. Nothing has been done to make it easy for people to get to the park. It is near the eastern end of the island. The boat landing is on the bay side of the island. The beach is a mile and a half away.

Primitive camping is allowed on the beach. There are a few chemical toilets, no electricity and no telephone. Only anglers and determined beachcombers in good health should come here.

The lighthouse in the park was built in 1872 to replace an earlier one built in 1852. The light marked the entrance to Pass Cavallo and Matagorda Bay. Ships bound to and from Indianola came this way until Indianola blew away in 1886. Boats still come this way, bound to and from Port O'Connor and Port Lavaca, but there are better navigation aids now. The last lighthouse keeper here retired in 1956 when the light was automated. The Coast Guard still keeps a light burning, but it is not a beacon. The old beacon lens is now on display in the Calhoun County Museum in Port Lavaca.

No hunting is allowed in the park. The plan is to allow hunting of waterfowl in the marshlands in the wildlife management areas during hunting seasons, but be sure to check with the superintendent.

For more information

There are no reservations to be made, but you can get more information about the park by writing to the Superintendent, Matagorda Island State Park, Box 117, Port O'Connor, TX 77982 or by calling (512) 983-2215.

Other places to see

The Aransas National Wildlife Refuge is in Austwell, 45 miles southwest of Port O'Connor.

Texas Fisherman editor Larry Bozka, left, hooks a trout in Espiritu Santo Bay off Matagorda Island Wildlife Conservation Area and State Park. He favors gold or silver spoons for trout or redfish. The spring and fall are the best times for redfish, trout and flounder here. There is a deep hole near here, called Army Hole, where redfish congregate in the winter.

COPANO BAY STATE FISHING PIER

State Highway 35 at Copano Bay, 6 miles north of Fulton in Aransas County, 41 miles northeast of Corpus Christi. Fee: $1 per rod

This causeway was recycled when a new causeway was built. Only part of the old causeway is still standing at the Port Lavaca State Fishing Pier. All of the old causeway is still in place here. It is close alongside the new bridge. Parking is plentiful. The fishing pier is operated by a concessionaire. He also has bait and fishing equipment for sale.

The fees are the same as those at the other two state fishing piers — $1 per rod or pole or thrownet each 24 hours.

For more information

You can get more information from the concessionaire at Box 39, Fulton, TX 78358. The phone number is (512) 729-8633.

Other places to see

Other places of interest nearby are Goose Island State Recreation Area, 3 miles from the north end of the fishing pier on Park Road 13; Aransas National Wildlife Refuge, entrance 25 miles northeast off F.M. 2040 south of Austwell; and Fulton Mansion State Historic Structure on the waterfront at Fulton, just south of the south end of the fishing pier.

Left: Anglers catch croaker, sand trout, sheepshead and gaff-top with dead bait at the Copano Bay State Fishing Pier. *Texas Fisherman* editor Larry Bozka says the best bet for fishermen in search of speckled trout is to fish live shrimp under the lights, in the spring and fall.

Opposite: The Fulton Mansion has the appearance of a masonry building. It actually was built with heavy planks, stacked board on board.

FULTON MANSION STATE HISTORIC STRUCTURE

On Fulton Beach Road just east of State Highway 35 between Fulton and Rockport in Aransas County, 36 miles northeast of Corpus Christi. Fees: adults $1, children 25¢

This house illustrates how well the really rich could live in this part of the world before most people had achieved the basic necessities. The Comanches still ruled a large part of northwest Texas when George and Harriet Fulton started building this mansion in 1874. Ordinary Texans had not even dreamed of indoor plumbing or central heat, but George and Harriet Fulton were not ordinary Texans.

George Fulton came to Texas from Philadelphia in 1837. He stayed long enough to meet and marry Harriet and then they went back East. George took up engineering. Harriet was the daughter of Henry Smith. He had been provisional governor of Texas in 1835 and he was a big landowner. Harriet inherited most of Smith's property when he died in 1851. George and Harriet came back to Texas after the Civil War to manage her estate. Much of the land was here on the coast. They started raising cattle and did very well.

The Fultons had plenty of money and George had plenty of advanced ideas from his days as an engineer when they got ready to build their home. This house was

built with a concrete foundation and basement, bathtubs and flush toilets, gas lights and a central heating system.

The Fultons lived here until George died in 1893. Harriet moved to Ohio then and the mansion was sold. It changed hands several times and suffered considerably from neglect until the Parks and Wildlife Department bought it for $150,000 in 1976. The grounds had been used as a mobile home park for several years before 1976 and the crumbling mansion was the social center.

The mansion is crumbling no more. The Parks and Wildlife Department has spent more money here than the Fultons did. The building has been carefully and completely restored. It has been furnished approximately the way it was furnished in the 1880s. The records survived; so the parks people knew what items the Fultons bought and where they bought them.

The Fulton mansion may be the best example of the Parks and Wildlife Department's new concern with authentic restoration of important buildings. The work took five years.

There is no charge for admission to the grounds here. The guided tours of the mansion are $1 for adults and 25 cents for children between 6 and 12. There is no charge for children under 6. Groups of more than 10 should make arrangements in advance. The mansion is open Wednesdays through Sundays from 9 a.m. to noon and 1 p.m. to 4 p.m.

For more information

The phone number for arranging tours is (512) 729-0386. The mailing address is Superintendent, Fulton Mansion, P.O. Box 1859, Fulton, TX 78358.

Other places to see

Some other places you may want to see in this area are Goose Island State Recreation Area, 11 miles north off State Highway 35; Aransas National Wildlife Refuge, 38 miles north off F.M. 2040; Mustang Island State Park, 22 miles south on Park Road 53 off State Highway 361; Padre Island National Seashore and the city of Corpus Christi.

This tree in the Goose Island State Recreation Area is certified to be the biggest coastal live oak in Texas. The Texas Forest Service estimates it is at least 1,000 years old.

GOOSE ISLAND STATE RECREATION AREA

On Park Road 13, off State Highway 35 at Lamar in Aransas County, 44 miles northeast of Corpus Christi. Entrance fee: $2 per car

This is an old park on a site with some history. Part of the park is on a peninsula between St. Charles Bay and Copano Bay. Part of it is on a small island just off the peninsula. The island has been called Goose Island as long as anyone can remember because wild geese used to winter on it before the tourists came. The peninsula was originally called Point Lookout. The story is that the Comanches used the peninsula as a rendezvous point during some of their excursions to the coast. The last Comanche raid in this part of the state occurred at Linnville in what is now Calhoun County in 1841. The peninsula here was being called Lamar Peninsula by that time. James Byrne had established a little community in 1838 and named it for Mirabeau Lamar. Sam Colt and his brother bought the townsite, the peninsula and Goose Island in 1856. They planned a big real estate development, but the plans were abandoned after Sam died in 1862.

Goose Island Recreation Area is now surrounded by real estate developments. The fishing camps and trailer parks on this part of the coast are rapidly being replaced by more expensive motels and condominium developments.

The state acquired Goose Island and 167 acres on Lamar Peninsula from various individuals in the early 1930s. The original improvements were built by the CCC in cooperation with the National Park Service. This is one of the parks most favored

by winter Texans. There are 45 campsites scattered along the water's edge on Goose Island. These have water, electricity, table, grill and a shade shelter. These sites are $6 a day. There are 57 campsites with water, electricity, table and grill in a wooded area on the mainland for $6 a night and 25 tent campsites for $4 a night, plus a group tent camping area.

The park has 29 individual picnic sites. A recreation hall accommodates up to 75 people and rents at $40 a day or $70 overnight. Restrooms near the camping areas all have showers. There is a boat ramp and a long, lighted fishing pier off the end of Goose Island.

This section of the coast is a birding hot spot. The birds most often seen here are gulls and terns, spotted sandpipers, willets, kildeer, great blue herons, Louisiana herons and the common and snowy egrets. Park headquarters has a bird checklist.

The entrance to the Aransas National Wildlife Refuge is about 30 miles north of here, but the southern end is just across St. Joseph's Bay from this park. The best place to see the whooping cranes the refuge is famous for is from the sightseeing boat *Whooping Crane*. This boat operates from a dock at the Sea Gun Inn at Park Road 13 and State Highway 35 when the whooping cranes are here (October to April).

For more information

You can get more information about Goose Island State Recreation Area by writing the Superintendent at Star Rt. 1, Box 105, Rockport, TX 78382 or by calling (512) 729-2858. Reservations are always advisable, especially at popular parks like this one.

Other places to see

Some other sights in this area are Fulton Mansion State Historic Structure, 11 miles south on Fulton Beach Road between Fulton and Rockport; Texas Parks and Wildlife Marine Lab and Aquarium, Rockport Turning Basin; Mustang Island State Park, 33 miles south on Park Road 53 off State Highway 361; and Corpus Christi and the Padre Island National Seashore.

Mustang Island State Park is one of the two or three most popular parks in the state system. But it is seldom really crowded.

MUSTANG ISLAND STATE PARK

On Park Road 53, 14 miles south of Port Aransas on Mustang Island in Nueces County, 22 miles east of Corpus Christi
Entrance fee: $2 per car

    This is one of the more popular state parks because it has a lot of open beach and it is close to Corpus Christi. Mustang Island is immediately north of Padre Island separated only by the narrow Corpus Christi Pass. You can get onto the island from State Highway 361 and the free ferry at Port Aransas or by taking the causeway from Corpus Christi and turning north on Park Road 53.

    The Parks and Wildlife Department bought the 3,790 acres for this park in 1972 after some prolonged and spirited discussions about the price. The department paid about $1,000 an acre and got five and a half miles of beach frontage. About half the frontage is undeveloped open beach. The rest is set up for picnicking and camping.

    There is a bathhouse near the park headquarters and there are 100 picnic sites with shade shelters. A campground near the picnic area has 48 campsites with water and electrical connections for $6 a night. A beach camping area extends

about a mile and a half south of the bathhouse. Chemical toilets, showers and water taps are provided at intervals along with 300 individual campsites at $4 a night.

A good many people come to the beach to do nothing, but many come to swim or fish. This park offers a fine swimming beach and pretty good fishing. A water exchange pass cuts across the island just north of the park headquarters. Rock jetties extend out into the Gulf on both sides of the pass entrance. Anglers often find action here.

For more information

The address for reservations or additional information is Superintendent, Mustang Island State Park, Box 326, Port Aransas, TX 78373. The phone number is (512) 749-5246.

Other places to see

The Padre Island National Seashore is 14 miles south of here, with 66 miles of open beach. A county park is located on the beach just north of the National Seashore headquarters. The city of Corpus Christi is across Corpus Christi Bay from Mustang Island Park, about 22 miles by road. Lake Corpus Christi State Recreation Area is about 60 miles northwest of this park. The Fulton Mansion State Historic Structure is about 33 miles northeast. The Goose Island State Recreation Area is about 42 miles north.

The Port Isabel Lighthouse was built in 1852 on land the government didn't bother to buy until 1894. It has been out of service since 1905 and a state park since 1952.

PORT ISABEL LIGHTHOUSE STATE HISTORIC STRUCTURE

On State Highway 100 in Port Isabel in Cameron County, 168 miles south of Corpus Christi. Fees: adults $1, children 25¢

This old lighthouse has been here since 1852. It has been a state park since 1952.

The federal government built this lighthouse on part of a site Gen. Zachary Taylor had used as a base in the early stages of the Mexican War in 1846. Washington was surprised to learn in 1888 that the government had never owned the land. There was a lot of negotiating before the owners and the government finally came to terms in 1894.

Port Isabel changed hands more than once during the Civil War. The light was extinguished, but Union and Confederate troops both used the tower as a lookout post at different times.

There once were 15 lamps and 21 reflectors in the tower. The light they made could be seen 16 miles away. The Coast Guard closed this lighthouse in 1905. The

government sold it in 1927. The state got it in 1947 as a gift from Lon C. Hill, Jr. Hill's father was the founder of Harlingen.

The Parks Board restored the tower and enlarged the area at the top to accommodate visitors. You can pose for pictures with the tower, as a lot of people do, without paying a fee. The fee for touring the interior and climbing the spiral staircase is $1 for adults and 25 cents for children, 6 to 12. No fee is collected from visitors with annual permits or senior citizens' passports.

For more information

You can get more information from the Superintendent, Port Isabel Lighthouse State Historic Structure, Box 863, Port Isabel, TX 78578. The phone number is (512) 943-1172.

Other places to see

Nearby places are South Padre Island across the causeway, Brownsville (29 miles southwest) and Matamoros across the Rio Grande.

The old causeway between Port Isabel and the southern end of Padre Island has been turned into a fishing pier. Anglers get speckled trout, sand trout, croaker, sheepshead, gaff-tops and flounder here. The pier is operated by a concessionaire.

QUEEN ISABELLA STATE FISHING PIER

On State Highway 100 at the south end of South Padre Island in Cameron County, 169 miles south of Corpus Christi. Fee: $1 per rod

This is another case where the Parks and Wildlife Department has salvaged an old causeway for recreation. There is a new causeway. The old one is a fishing pier. There is a concessionaire in charge. He collects a fee of $1 per rod or pole or thrownet. The fee entitles you to fish for 24 hours. The concessionaire also keeps tackle and bait for sale.

The old causeway was only a few feet above sea level with a section in the center that had to be opened every time a boat or barge wanted to pass. It was inadequate once the condominium boom got started on South Padre.

BRAZOS ISLAND STATE RECREATION AREA

Off State Highway 4 at Boca Chica, 24 miles east of Brownsville in Cameron County, 185 miles south of Corpus Christi. No fee

Two hundred and seventeen acres on the beach here were transferred from the General Land Office to the State Parks Board in 1957. The legislature approved the transfer because the people of Brownsville wanted a park. They are still waiting.

No improvements have been made at Brazos Island. There is no staff and no entrance fee. People can camp on the beach and they do. They have to bring everything they need with them. They do not always carry their litter away with them. It may be your kind of place. It is not often crowded.

Top: Brazos Island State Park is a beach much like the beach on South Padre Island but a lot less accessible. State Highway 4 is the only way in and out. A Parks and Wildlife Department sign on the road warns visitors before they get here to expect nothing. The site is leased to Cameron County and there are no plans for improvements, but picnicking and camping are allowed.

Opposite: Hikers on the nature trail in Bentsen Rio Grade Valley State Park get an idea what this area was like before the farmers started clearing and plowing it. People from the Middle West do most of the camping here in winter months.

BENTSEN-RIO GRANDE VALLEY STATE PARK

On F.M. 2062 off Loop 374, southwest of Mission in Hidalgo County on the Mexican border, 188 miles south of Corpus Christi. Entrance fee: $2 per car

Lloyd Bentsen's parents gave this park to the state in 1944. It is 587 acres with all the natural vegetation this area had before agriculture became so big here. The property has frontage on the Rio Grande and portions of two resacas. A resaca is a lake left behind when a river changes its channel. They are usually called oxbow lakes in English, but the Spanish had already named these in this part of the world before we got here.

This is one of the parks preferred by winter Texans. Birdwatchers are drawn here because there are birds here found in very few other places in the United States. Some of these birds are the grey hawk, clay-colored robin, rose-throated becard, ringed kingfisher and varied bunting. Bird checklists are available at park headquarters. The park has a hiking trail, nature trail, boat ramp, fish-cleaning table and playground. There are 10 picnic sites and 142 campsites. Seventy-seven of the campsites have full trailer hookups — water, electricity, sewer connections, table and grill. The other 65 sites have tables and grills but no hookups. These

sites are $4 a night. Those with full hookups are $7 a night.

The park has one group shelter, accommodating 100 people for rent at $8 a day for groups under 25, $16 for groups of more than 25. There is a sanitary dump. Restrooms in the camping areas have showers.

For more information

You can make reservations or get more information about the Bentsen-Rio Grande Valley State Park by calling (512) 585-1107 or by writing the Superintendent at Box 988, Mission, TX 78572.

Other places to see

Other places you may want to see here, besides the citrus groves, are the last manually operated international ferry, 18 miles west at Los Ebanos on F.M. 886; La Lomita Mission on F.M. 1016 south of Mission; the Hudson Auto Museum on U.S. 83 in west McAllen; and the Confederate Air Force Museum at the airport in Harlingen.

Top: Fishing and boating are allowed in the small lakes, or resacas, in the Bentsen-Rio Grande Valley State Park, but swimming is not permitted.

Opposite: The busy season at the Bentsen-Rio Grande Valley State Park is the winter season, from December through April. Most of the campers then are from the Middle West.

FALCON STATE RECREATION AREA

On Park Road 46, off F.M. 2098, 15 miles north of Roma in Starr and Zapata counties, 241 miles southwest of Corpus Christi.
Entrance fee: $2 per car

Falcon Lake was built by the United States and Mexican governments. It was finished in 1953 and dedicated by President Eisenhower and Mexican President Adolfo Ruiz Cortines. The lake is managed by the International Boundary and Water Commission. The state leased the 563 acres for this park from the commission in 1954. The park opened in 1965.

This is one of our biggest lakes. It attracts sailors, swimmers, skiers and fishermen. The fish caught here are mostly black bass, white bass, striped bass, crappie and catfish. The park is about two miles above the dam. There is a boat ramp, dock and fish-cleaning tables.

The park has its own airstrip with an asphalt runway 3,000 feet long. There are 24 screened shelters for rent here at $8 a night. There are 31 campsites with water, electricity, table, grill and shade shelter for $6 a night; and 31 trailer sites with water, electricity, sewer connections, table and grill for $7 a night. The 73 picnic sites have tables, grills and shade shelters and 55 of these sites are rented as campsites during the winter months at $4 a night.

The restrooms in the camping areas have showers and some have laundry tubs. There are two sanitary dumps and a recreation building that can be rented for group events. It will accommodate up to 75 people and rents for $40 a day.

This area attracts an assortment of birds. Most of those common to the chaparral country and the Chihuahuan Desert are seen here as well as some less common varieties like the chachalaca, brown jay and green kingfisher in the forest below the dam.

For more information

You can make reservations or get more information about Falcon State Recreation Area from the Superintendent, P.O. Box 48, Falcon Heights, TX 78545. The phone number is (512) 848-5327.

Other places to see

You may want to see a little bit of Mexico while you are here. F.M. 2098 will take you across the dam to Nuevo Guerrero. This is a new Mexican town built when the lake flooded old Guerrero. The lake also flooded the town of Falcon on the Texas side. The people there moved to Falcon Village and Falcon Heights. You can drive south from Nuevo Guerrero to Cuidad Mier and cross the toll bridge back into Texas at Roma, or you can continue on the Mexican side down to Cuidad Camargo and cross the toll bridge there to Rio Grande City. Roma goes back to the 1760s and looks more Mexican than Texan. An old Army post called Fort Ringgold is one of the sights in Rio Grande City. It is off U.S. 83 on the east side of town. Crossing the border is pretty simple unless you are carrying something you should not be carrying. You do not absolutely have to have a Mexican tourist card if you are not going into the interior, but it will make things simpler. Check your car insurance to be sure you are covered south of the border. You can buy temporary Mexican insurance almost anywhere on the border if you need to. Get it on the Texas side. Be sure you have proof that you own your car, too.

Cuidad Mier figured in Texas history. A small Texas force raided the town in December, 1842. They thought things were going their way until a superior Mexican force showed up. The Texans put up a fight and then surrendered. Some of them escaped while they were being marched to Mexico City. They were recaptured and every tenth man was executed outside Salado in the infamous black bean episode.

The Falcon State Recreation Area has frontage on Falcon Lake and an air strip.

229

INDEX
The State Parks of Texas
(*Park not yet open to public)

Abilene State Recreation Area: 76
Acton State Historic Site: 62
Admiral Nimitz State Historical Park: 184
*Arroyo Colorado Site: 199
Atlanta State Recreation Area: 102
Balmorhea State Recreation Area: 40
Bastrop State Park: 168
Battleship Texas Historic Site: 128
Bentsen-Rio Grande Valley State Park: 225
Big Spring State Recreation Area: 51
Blanco State Recreation Area: 180
Bonham State Recreation Area: 94
Brazos Bend State Park: 135
Brazos Island State Recreation Area: 224
Bryan Beach State Recreation Area: 132
Buescher State Park: 166
Caddo Lake State Park: 103
Caddoan Mounds State Historic Site: 113
Caprock Canyons State Park: 58
Cassells Boykin State Park: 147
*Choke Canyon State Park: 199
Cleburne State Recreation Area: 65
Confederate Reunion Grounds: 123
Copano Bay State Fishing Pier: 214
Copper Breaks State Park: 80
Daingerfield State Park: 100
*Davis Hill Site: 125
Davis Mountains State Park: 37
Dinosaur Valley State Park: 63
*Eagle Mountain Lake Park: 61
Eisenhower Birthplace State Historic Site: 92
Eisenhower State Recreation Area: 90
Enchanted Rock State Natural Area: 186
Fairfield Lake State Recreation Area: 117
Falcon State Recreation Area: 227
Fannin Battleground State Historic Site: 207
*Fanthorp Inn State Historic Site: 125
Fort Griffin State Historical Park: 78
Fort Lancaster State Historic Site: 44
Fort Leaton State Historic Site: 35
Fort McKavett State Historic Site: 48
Fort Parker State Recreation Area: 119
Fort Richardson State Historical Park: 83
Franklin Mountains State Park: 32
Fulton Mansion State Historic Structure: 215
Galveston Island State Park: 129
Garner State Park: 194
Goliad State Historical Park: 204
Goose Island State Recreation Area: 217
Governor Hogg Shrine State Historical Park: 98
Guadalupe River State Park: 160
Hill Country State Natural Area: 190
Hueco Tanks State Historical Park: 33
Huntsville State Park: 143
Inks Lake State Park: 176
Jeff Davis State Recreation Area: 67
Jim Hogg State Historical Park: 108
Jose Antonio Navarro State Historic Site: 158
Kerrville State Recreation Area: 188
Lake Arrowhead State Recreation Area: 82

*Lake Bob Sandlin Site: 89
Lake Brownwood State Recreation Area: 74
Lake Colorado City State Recreation Area: 50
Lake Corpus Christi State Recreation Area: 200
*Lake Houston State Park: 125
*Lake Lewisville State Recreation Area: 89
Lake Livingston State Recreation Area: 145
Lake Mineral Wells State Park: 87
Lake Somerville State Recreation Area: 141
*Lake Tawakoni Site: 89
Lake Texana State Recreation Area: 209
Lake Whitney State Recreation Area: 68
*Lakeview State Recreation Area: 89
Landmark Inn State Historic Site: 196
Lipantilan State Historic Site: 202
Lockhart State Recreation Area: 170
Longhorn Cavern State Park: 174
Lost Maples State Natural Area: 192
Lyndon B. Johnson State Historical Park: 182
MacKenzie State Recreation Area: 52
Magoffin Home State Historic Site: 30
Martin Creek Lake State Recreation Area: 105
Martin Dies Jr. State Park: 148
Matagorda Island State Park: 212
McKinney Falls State Park: 172
Meridian State Recreation Area: 70
Mission Tejas State Historical Park: 115
Monahans Sandhills State Park: 42
Monument Hill-Kreische Brewery: 164
Mother Neff State Park: 72
Mustang Island State Park: 219
Old Fort Parker State Historic Site: 121
Palmetto State Park: 162
Palo Duro Canyon State Park: 54
Pedernales Falls State Park: 178
Port Isabel Lighthouse State Historic Structure: 221
Port Lavaca State Fishing Pier: 211
Possum Kingdom State Recreation Area: 85
*Purtis Creek Site: 89
Queen Isabella State Fishing Pier: 223
*Rancho de las Cabras State Historic Site: 155
Resaca de Palma Park: 199
Rusk/Palestine State Park: 110
Sabine Pass Battleground Historical Park: 150
Sam Bell Maxey House State Historic Structure: 96
San Jacinto Battleground Historical Park: 126
San Jose Mission State Historic Site: 156
Sea Rim State Park: 152
*Sebastopol House State Historic Structure: 155
Seminole Canyon State Historical Park: 46
*Sheldon Site State Recreation Area: 125
*South Llano River Site: 29
*Starr Mansion State Historic Site: 89
Stephen F. Austin Historical Park: 137
Texas State Railroad Historical Park: 110
Tips State Recreation Area: 203
Tyler State Park: 106
Varner-Hogg Historical Park: 133
*Village Creek Park Site: 125
Washington-On-The-Brazos Historical Park: 139

ACKNOWLEDGEMENTS

The author and publisher are indebted to the men and women of the Texas Parks and Wildlife Department for advice and assistance. Special thanks to Bill Reaves, Leroy Williamson, Bill Scruggs, David Baxter, Susie Gonzalez, Bill Collins, Mike Herring, Glen Mills and Sue Moss. Thanks also to Melissa Locke Roberts of the Texas State Library in Austin, Doris Glasser and the staff of the Texas and Local History Room of the Houston Public Library, *Texas Fisherman* editor Larry Bozka and Judy King of Houston.

Some of the publications worthy of recommendation to readers wishing more information are:

Texas Parks and Wildlife magazine is a beautifully photographed color publication, useful for anyone interested in hiking, camping, fishing and picnicking. It is published monthly by the Texas Parks and Wildlife Department, 4200 Smith School Road in Austin, TX 78744. Subscriptions are $8 per year.

Texas Highways magazine is a good source of information about seasonal events in Texas. Also in color, it is published monthly by the Department of Highways and Public Transportation, P.O. Box 5016 in Austin, TX 78763. A year's subscription is $10.

Gene Kirkley's book, *Texas Rivers and Streams,* is published by the Lone Star Books Division of Gulf Publishing Company in Houston.

The Department of Highways and Public Transportation publishes a free book about Texas attractions under the title *Texas, Live the Legend.* It is available from the Department of Highways and Public Transportation, Travel and Information Division, Box 5064 in Austin, TX 78763. Free Texas highway maps, updated every year, can be obtained from the same source. This same division of the highway department publishes a free directory listing all the public campgrounds managed by federal, state and local governments in Texas.

The truck drivers all know, but some other travelers don't know, that they can stop free for up to 24 hours in any of the highway department's roadside parks. No tents or shelters can be put up, though.

PHOTO CREDITS

The author and publisher wish to express their gratitude to *Texas Parks and Wildlife* magazine and their photographers for permitting the reproduction of color photographs from their collections. The black and white photographs were made by the author with these exceptions: Donald Beene of El Paso made the photos of the Magoffin Home and Franklin Mountains State Park; Randy Stark of Quitaque made the photo of Caprock Canyons State Park.

Color photos by *Texas Parks and Wildlife* photographers:

Ernest Marsh, 11
Glen Mills, 12 (above), 13, 17 (above), 19 (below)
Bill Reaves, 16, 18, 20, 22
Jim Whitcomb, 21 (below)
Leroy Williamson, 12 (below), 14, 15, 17 (below), 19 (above), 21 (above), 23, 24, 25, 26

Cover Photograph: Matagorda Lighthouse by Bill Reaves

Back Cover Photo: Ray Miller on the bridge of Mike Harper's *Dogwatch*, en route to Matagorda Island — by Delton Simmons